Violin

# The Magic of Music Theory

## Book 2

### Kristin Campbell

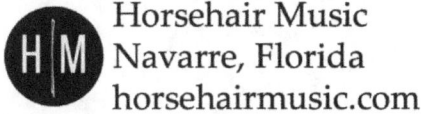

Horsehair Music
Navarre, Florida
horsehairmusic.com

Book 2 Violin ISBN 978-1-959514-17-6; Library of Congress Number: 2024919592
Book 2 Viola  ISBN 978-1-959514-19-0; Library of Congress Number: 2024919591
Book 2 Cello  ISBN 978-1-959514-20-6; Library of Congress Number: 2024919590

This book is dedicated to Laura Crawford and Charles Regauer, directors of the Centenary Suzuki School in Shreveport, Louisiana. Thank you for welcoming me into your Suzuki family and giving me a platform to teach theory to string students.

Special thanks to Ruth Coleman for her editorial help. Thanks to all the students who have tested out these pages and activities.

**Graphics:**
Cover Design: Christiana Hudson and Kristin Campbell
Hand image by www.vectorportal.com
String instrument, fingerboard and bow images by Kristin Campbell
All other images from www.freesvg.com

**To the student:**

Welcome to the Magic of Music Theory! Did you know that when you write things on paper it helps you remember them? This book is to help you remember things that you have learned in your lesson by writing them down. This will help you become a better musician. If you have any questions, be sure to ask your teacher. When you finish this book, you will know and understand more about how music is made. It's like magic, the magic of music theory!

**To the practice partner:**

You are the violin hero. Practicing isn't always fun, and it's not always easy. But in this journey of learning to play the violin, you get to walk alongside a child and give them the gift of music that will last for a lifetime.

My hope is that this series helps your student understand how music is written beginning with the basics and building up from there. If there is a concept or lesson that is hard for your student, don't be afraid to help and lead the student to the answer. There are many details to think about in music theory and the student may not grasp it all the first time it is introduced. That's ok! You will find a lot of review built in throughout the book and they will begin to understand and remember. This is the process of learning.

You can choose to do the lesson at the end of one practice session, or you could choose to divide it up with just a little bit each day. It's up to you. Ask your teacher if they would like to do the "What Do You Hear?" pages in the lesson or if you should do them at home. You can access videos online or download free mp3 tracks with each question played on a violin. The answers for each question are given on the video/ track, so that the student gets immediate feedback in the learning process. I hope you enjoy the magic of learning music theory.

**To the teacher:**

I created this series realizing my violin students were not getting music theory. I needed something they could do at home, so I wasn't giving up valuable lesson time. By writing and drawing, I wanted to engage a different part of their thinking in the music learning process. Sometimes writing it on paper has helped them comprehend a concept. This series teaches students how to write and read music and relates it to the fingerboard.

In my own teaching, I assign a lesson to the student asking them to read and follow the instructions. The following week, I take a minute at the end of the lesson to look over their work. As a Suzuki teacher, I teach the student to play a concept on the instrument first. Then, the student learns to read the concept in a note reading book. Then, I use these theory workbooks to have the student write or draw the concept. Most often I choose to place a student in a workbook that is one or two levels below their playing and reading ability.

The aural skills pages, "What Do You Hear?" can be done in the lesson if you have time, or through online videos or mp3 tracks. The QR code on each page will take you to the online video. To download free mp3 tracks visit horsehairmusic.com. Suggested recordings are linked to online videos to listen to while doing the discover the composer pages, but you may select your favorite artist or recording to share with your student.

You can also find the games and flashcards as a pdf download at horsehairmusic.com. This allows you to download and print the games in color or print the flashcards on heavier cardstock.

# The Magic of Music Theory Series Guide

**Use this chart to help find the level that is right for your student.**

| Ages 6 & up Repertoire Book 1 | Ages 7 & up Repertoire Book 2 | Ages 7 & up Repertoire Late Book 2 & up | Ages 8 & up Repertoire Book 3 & up |
|---|---|---|---|
| **Magic of Music Theory: Primer** | **Magic of Music Theory: Book 1** | **Magic of Music Theory: Book 2** | **Magic of Music Theory: Book 3** |
| • Student has begun reading in school.<br>• Student is ready or has begun note reading.<br>• Student can write all letters of English alphabet.<br>• Introduces staff notes for 2 upper strings.<br>• After completion move to Book 1. | • Student is reading chapter books in school.<br>• Student knows the letter names for A and E string fingerboard notes.<br>• Student can read A and E String staff notes well.<br>• Student needs reinforcing of lower string staff reading.<br>• Student has played 1 octave scale beginning on an open string and is ready to learn to read and write major scale pattern.<br>• Student understands down and up bow concept.<br>• After completion move to Book 2. | • Student can read all staff notes in first position.<br>• Student understands how to play "high" and "low" fingers. Ready to learn how to write and draw chromatic staff pitches.<br>• Has played slurs and hooked bows. Ready to learn to write bowing in score.<br>• Has played 1 octave scales of C, G, D, A.<br>• Confident in reading note values.<br>• After completion move to Book 3. | • Student can easily read staff notes in first position in treble clef. Ready to learn reading in another clef.<br>• Can play and read eighth notes, sixteenth notes and triplets. Ready to learn to write these note values in simple and compound meters.<br>• Confident in understanding and counting simple meter. Ready to learn compound meter.<br>• Can play 1 octave scales in first position. Ready to learn writing key signatures.<br>• Understands basic bow markings – down, up, slur, staccato, hooked bow. |

# Table of Contents

# Lesson 1

The **string family** is made up of violin, viola, cello and double bass (pronounced "base" like baseball!). The smaller the instrument, the higher the notes it plays. The larger the instrument, the lower the notes it plays. A **string orchestra** is made up of only stringed instruments. A **symphony** [sim-phone-ee] **orchestra** adds brass, woodwind, and percussion instruments. The person who stands and waves his or her arms at the front is called the **conductor** or **maestro** [my-strow]. The conductor waves a stick called a **baton** to help everyone play together.

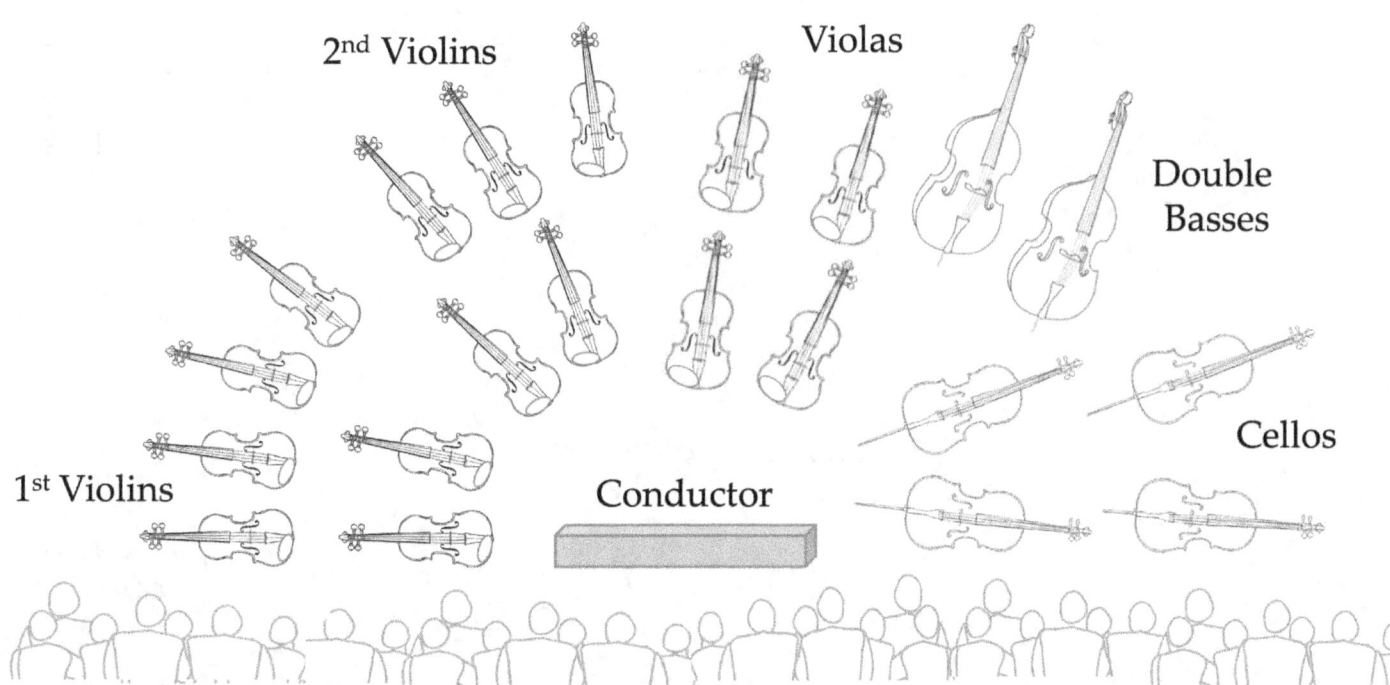

There are **sections** in the orchestra – 1st violins, 2nd violins, violas, cellos, and double basses. The 1st violins (or "firsts" for short) usually have the melody, and they play the higher part. Because we want the audience to hear the melody, the 1st violins have the most players in that section. The 2nd violins (or "seconds" for short) usually play harmony. Their part is usually a little lower than the 1st violin part. The violas play another harmony part usually lower than the 2nd violin. The cellos play a lower harmony part and usually the lowest pitches called the bass line. The double basses often play some of the same notes that the cellos play, but the notes sound even lower than the cellos.

1. Look at the picture above and write the number of players in each section in the blank.

      1st violins _____     2nd violins _____     Violas _____     Cellos _____     Basses _____

Which section has the most players? _____

Which section has the least number of players?_____

Why do you think that is? _____

# What do you hear? #1

Each section of the orchestra has a leader. Sometimes that person is called the **section leader,** or the **principle** of that section. The principle sits at the front of the section and makes decisions about how the section will bow the music. The first chair of the 1st violins is called the **concertmaster.** Before orchestras had conductors, the concertmaster was also the leader of the whole orchestra.

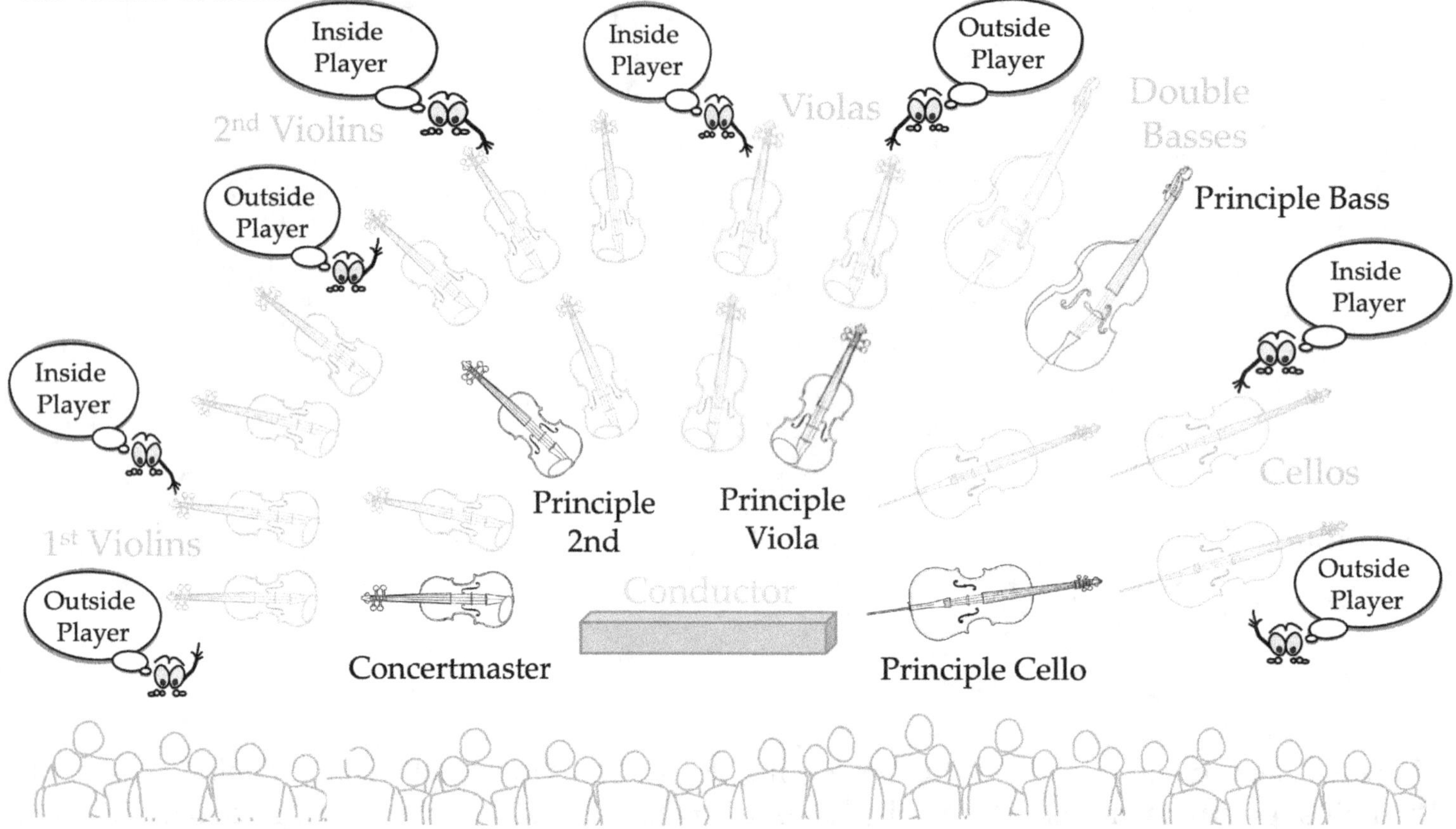

Most of the time, two players in each section share a music stand. The person sharing the stand with you is called your **stand partner.** The person sitting closest to the audience is the **outside player.** The person sitting closer to the back of the stage is called the **inside player.** The inside player always turns the pages.

1. Watch a video of a string orchestra playing Peter Warlock's *Capriol Suite*.

2. What is the name of the orchestra on the video? _____

3. Check the box for each thing you see or hear.

- ❑ Conductor
- ❑ 1st violins – how many?_____
- ❑ 2nd violins – how many?_____
- ❑ Violas – how many?_____
- ❑ Cellos – how many?_____
- ❑ Basses – how many?_____

- ❑ Concertmaster
- ❑ Stand Partners
- ❑ Page turns
- ❑ What section had the melody?

  _____

The Magic of Music Theory Book 2 - © 2025 Horsehair Music. Photocopying prohibited.

# Lesson 2

1. Draw a line from the term to the correct part of the violin and bow.

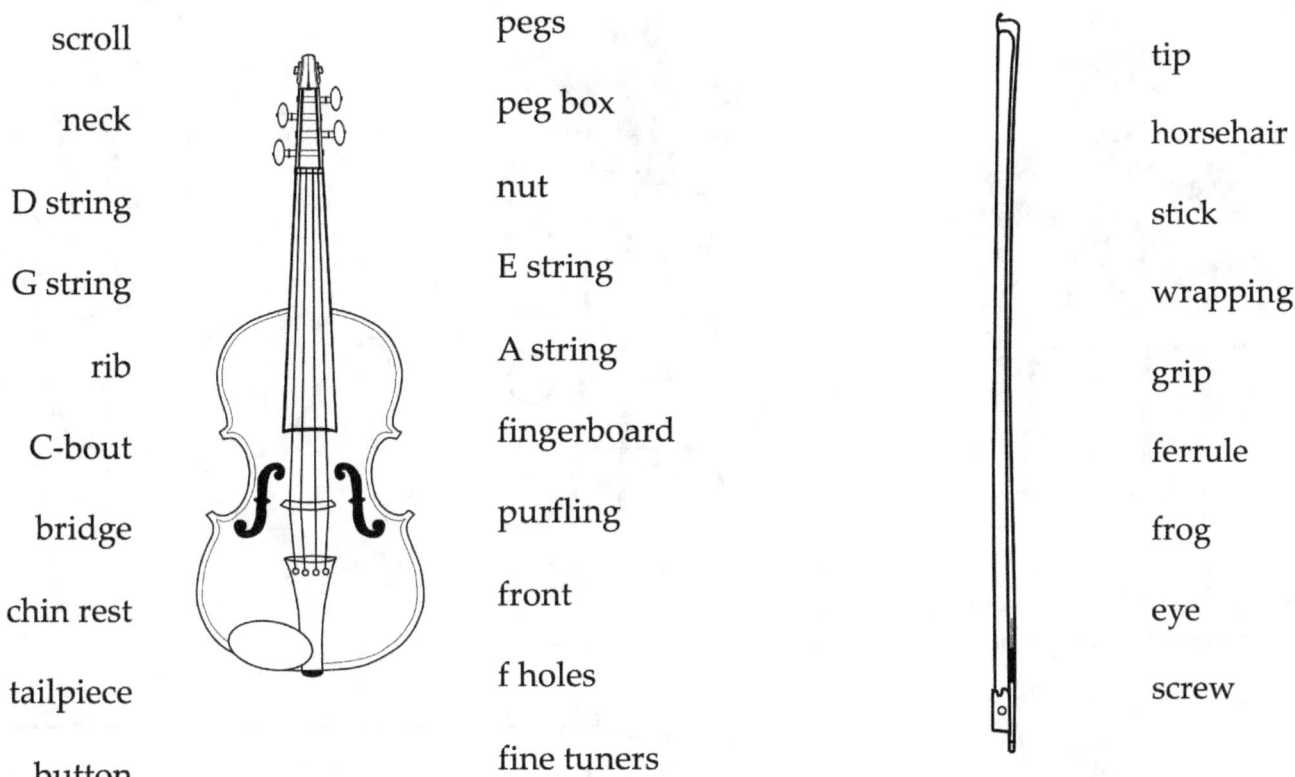

scroll

neck

D string

G string

rib

C-bout

bridge

chin rest

tailpiece

button

pegs

peg box

nut

E string

A string

fingerboard

purfling

front

f holes

fine tuners

tip

horsehair

stick

wrapping

grip

ferrule

frog

eye

screw

The parts of the bow are the same for all stringed instruments, and many parts of the violin are the same as the viola and cello. The viola and cello have different open strings than the violin, and the cello has an **endpin**. The endpin is the long metal rod that rests on the floor.

**Parts of the Cello**

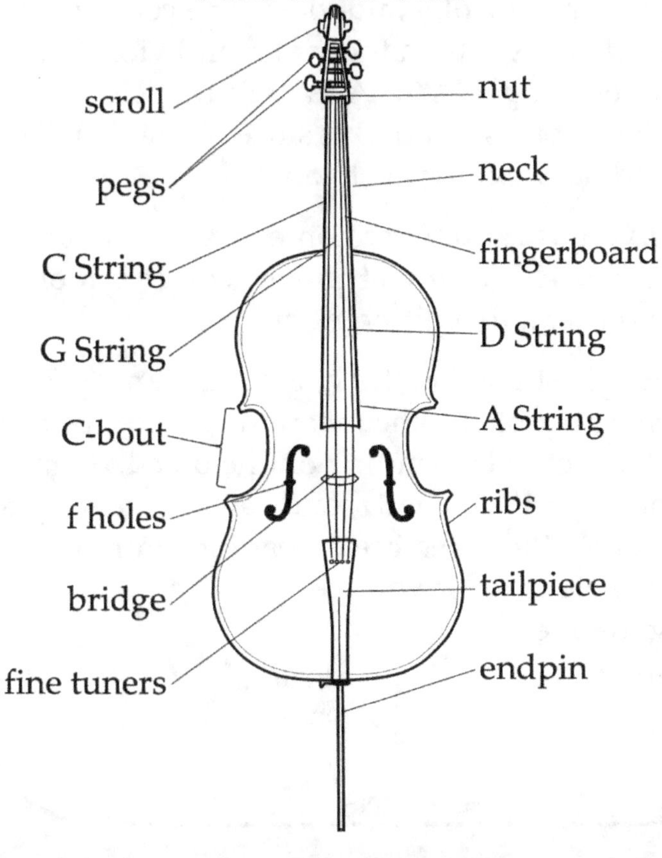

scroll

pegs

C String

G String

C-bout

f holes

bridge

fine tuners

nut

neck

fingerboard

D String

A String

ribs

tailpiece

endpin

2. Draw a line from the term to correct part.

scroll

pegs

C String

G String

C-bout

f holes

bridge

fine tuners

nut

neck

fingerboard

D String

A String

ribs

tailpiece

endpin

3. Write the open string letter for the violin in each house.

4. Write the finger numbers in each circle.

5. Write the correct finger number on each finger.

6. Write the letters in each house on the fingerboard.

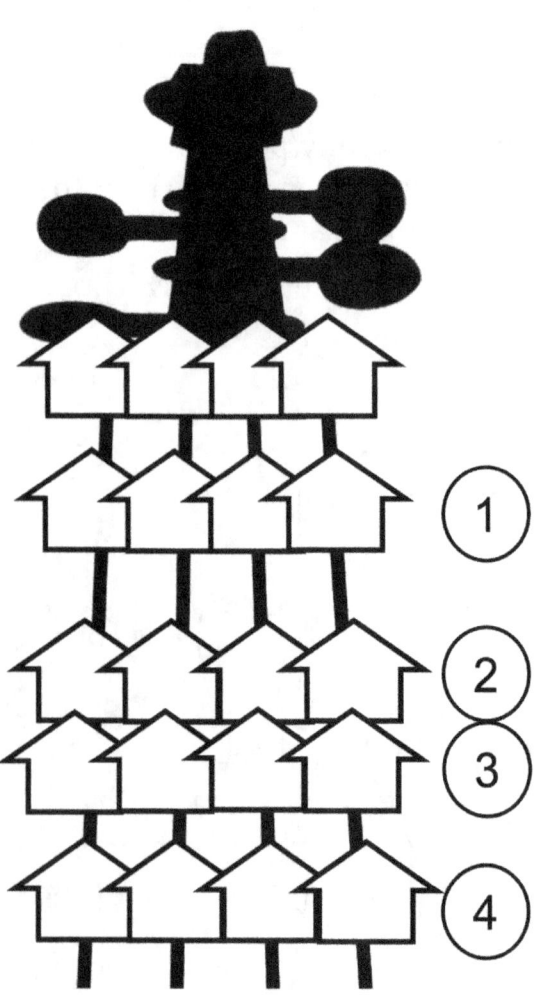

**? ? Did you know???**

The tuning note for an orchestra is called **A-440**. That means there are 440 vibration cycles in ONE SECOND!!!! The note that sounds at 440 hertz is "A." It is the same as "open A" for the violin and viola. The cello "open A" is 8 notes lower than the violin and viola "open A." The cello "open A" is A-220. That is 220 vibrations in one second. But since it is still an "A," cellos and basses can tune to an A-440.

If you use a tuner at home be sure the tuning note is set to 440. Your instrument will be out of tune if you set it to a different number.

The highest note on the violin is around 3520 hertz. Most people can hear sounds that range from 20 – 15,000 hertz. Depending on the breed, dogs can hear up to 40,000 hertz, and cats can hear up to 60,000 hertz. With such great hearing, your pet might be able to tell if you are playing in tune or out of tune!

# What do you hear? #2

Watch or listen to Concerto for Violin and Cello in B-flat Major, I. Allegro, RV 547 by Antonio Vivaldi. Every time the violin or cello has a solo, draw a tick mark under that instrument.

|  Solo Violin  |  Solo Cello  |
| --- | --- |
|  |  |

Answer as many questions as you can:

1. Was there a conductor? Yes or No _____

2. How do you think the players all stayed together? _____

_____

_____

3. How many 1st violins did you see? _____    4. How many 2nd violins did you see? _____

5. How many violas did you see? _____    6. How many cellos did you see? _____

7. How many double basses did you see? _____

8. How many people total were playing? _____

9. Was the orchestra set up in the same way as the diagram on p. 6? Yes or No _____

10. If the answer to question 9 was No, how was it different? _____

_____

# Lesson 3

The **staff** has 5 lines and 4 spaces. *Always* count the lines and spaces from bottom to top! Notes between two lines are **space notes**. Notes with a line through the middle are **line notes**.

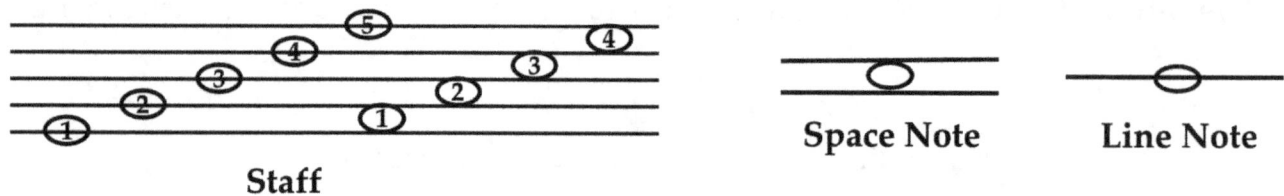

**Staff**

**Space Note**　　　**Line Note**

1. Trace each of the clefs. Then draw the clef on each empty staff below.

| Violins read music written in the **treble clef.** | Violas read music written in the **alto clef.** | Cellos read music written in the **bass clef.** |

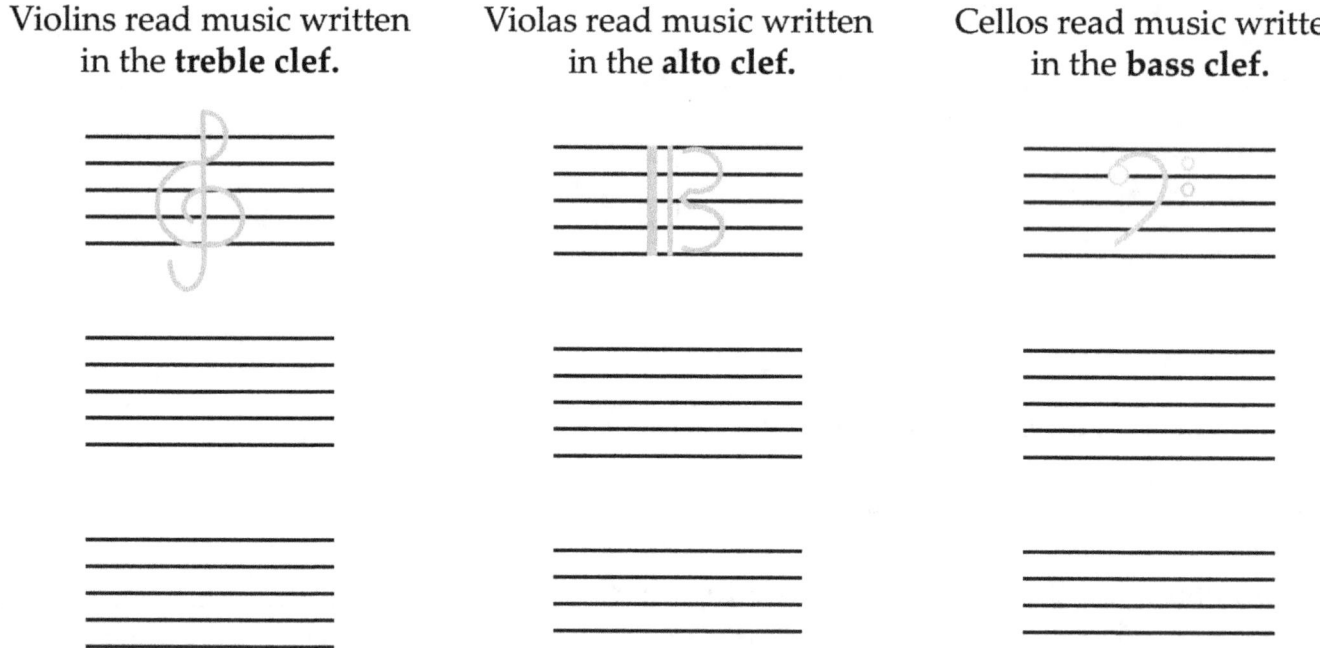

**?? *Did you know???*** The three clefs make reading music easier. Each note has a place on the staff, and we only have 5 lines and 4 spaces, we mostly use ledger line notes for the notes that violas and cellos play.

viola first position notes

cello first position notes

If cellists and violists had to read treble clef, many of their notes would be on ledger lines below the staff. That makes it hard to read to read quickly! By using different clefs, the notes move onto the staff. The alto clef moves the notes up 6 places on the staff. The bass clef moves the notes up 13 places on the staff. Using these two clefs allow more of the notes that violist and cellist play to be on the staff.

The Magic of Music Theory Book 2 - © 2025 Horsehair Music. Photocopying prohibited.

2. Draw the clef. Then draw the note that shows the clef's name on the empty staff.

**Treble Clef = G-Clef**

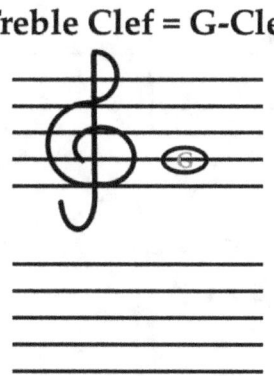

**Alto Clef = C-Clef**

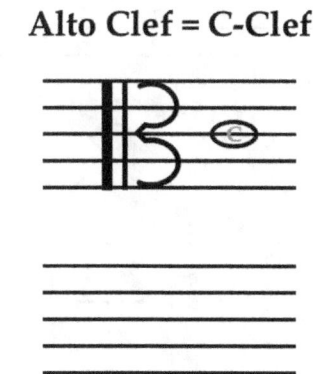

**Bass Clef = F-Clef**

3. Each fingerboard house has a matching note on the staff. Write the letters in each house on the fingerboard. Draw a treble clef on each staff. Then fill in the letter name and finger number for the notes on the staff.

Letter: __E__ ___ ___ ___ ___
Finger number: __0__ ___ ___ ___ ___

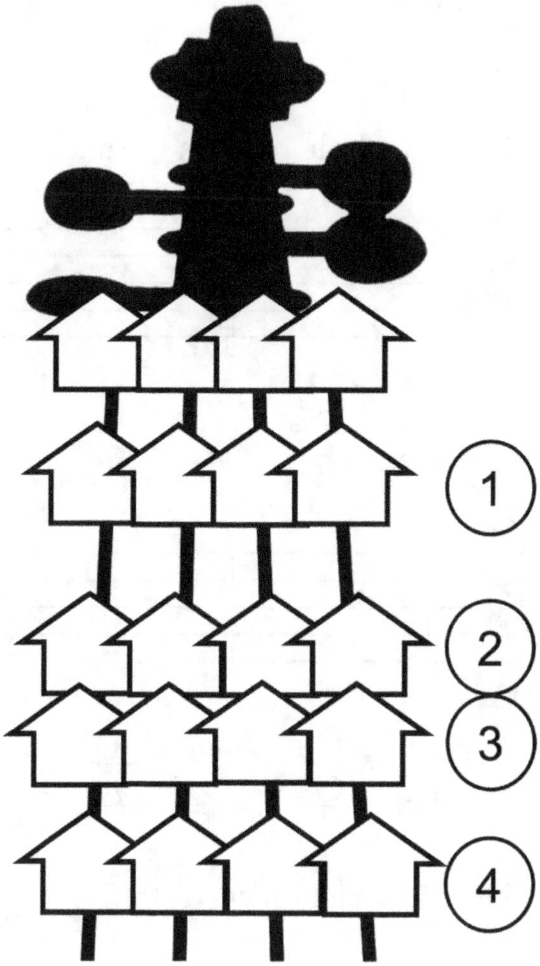

Letter: __A__ ___ ___ ___ ___
Finger number: __0__ ___ ___ ___ ___

Letter: __D__ ___ ___ ___ ___
Finger number: __0__ ___ ___ ___ ___

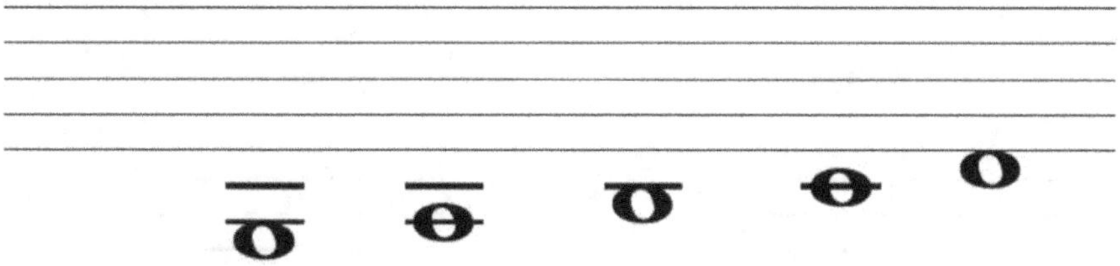

Letter: __G__ ___ ___ ___ ___
Finger number: __0__ ___ ___ ___ ___

① ② ③ ④

4. Write the letter name for each note. Then, write the string that it lives on.

Letter: ___      ___      ___      ___      ___

String: ___      ___      ___      ___      ___

Letter: ___      ___      ___      ___      ___

String: ___      ___      ___      ___      ___

5. Draw a whole note on the staff that matches the letter and the string.

| Letter: | F# | G | E | G# | B | E |
|---------|----|---|---|----|---|---|
| String: | E  | G | A | E  | G | D |

| Letter: | C | D | F# | C# | A | G |
|---------|---|---|----|----|---|---|
| String: | G | A | D  | A  | G | D |

6. Draw the clef on each staff.

Treble Clef           Alto Clef           Bass Clef

The Magic of Music Theory Book 2 - © 2025 Horsehair Music. Photocopying prohibited.

### Discover the Composers

Fill in the letter of the note to learn about the life of a great composer while you listen to  Serenade for String Orchestra, III. Scherzo: Allegro Vivace, by Teresa Carreño.

T__r__s__ __ __ rreño was ___rom Ven__zu__l__. She be___ an piano lessons

with her ___ ___ther. Her ___ ___mily ___mi___rat___ ___ to ___meri___ ___ when she

was 9. She per___ormed at the White House ___or A___r___h___m Lin___oln and later

for Woodrow Wilson! She ___omposed 75 works. Most w___r___ ___or piano. She wrote

2 works for strings, a strin___ qu___rt___t and S___r___n___ ___ ___ for string orchestra.

__ ___r__t__r on V___nus is n__m___ ___ ___ ___rr__ño ___ __t__r her.

7. Was this music fast or slow? _____

# Lesson 4

**Dynamics** means volume. We use Italian words for dynamics, telling how loud or soft to play.

$f$ = forte = loud          $mf$ = mezzo forte = medium loud

$p$ = piano = soft          $mp$ = mezzo piano = medium soft

The Italian word **mezzo**, means medium. (In Italian "zz" is pronounced quickly with "ts" sound. Like a soft sizzle.) **Mezzo forte** is a little softer than forte. And **mezzo piano** is a little softer than mezzo forte, but louder than piano.

To play something louder than forte, a composer will mark **fortissimo** [for-tiss-ee-mo]. This means VERY loud. The opposite of fortissimo is **pianissimo** [pee-an-iss-ee-mo]. Pianissimo means very soft. Pianissimo is softer than piano.

$ff$ = *fortissimo* = very loud          $pp$ = *pianissimo* = very soft

1. Write a dynamic sign on each sticky note in order from loudest to softest.

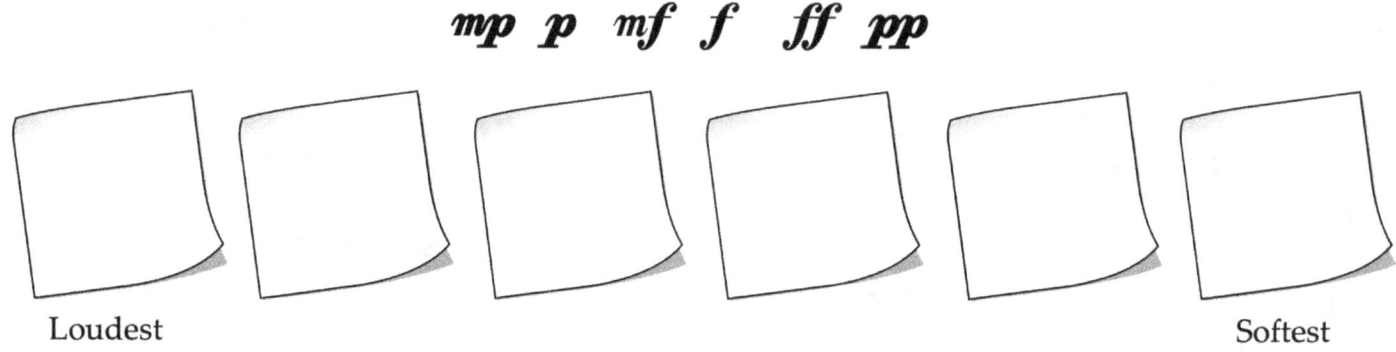

$mp$   $p$   $mf$   $f$   $ff$   $pp$

Loudest                                                      Softest

2. Write a dynamic sign in the blank that describes each picture.

A **crescendo** [creh-shen-dough] means to play gradually louder.  A **diminuendo** [di-min-u-ehn-dough] or **decrescendo** [day-creh-shen-dough] means to play gradually softer. The wide end of the symbol shows the loud end, and the point shows the soft end.

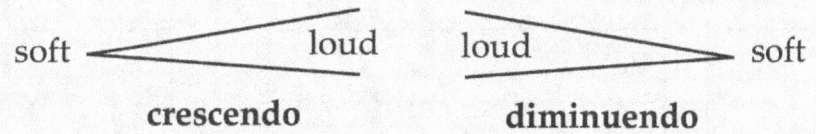

soft ◁——————— loud     loud ———————▷ soft

**crescendo**          **diminuendo**

Diminuendo and crescendo signs are always drawn under the staff.

3. Draw the correct symbol in the box above each term.

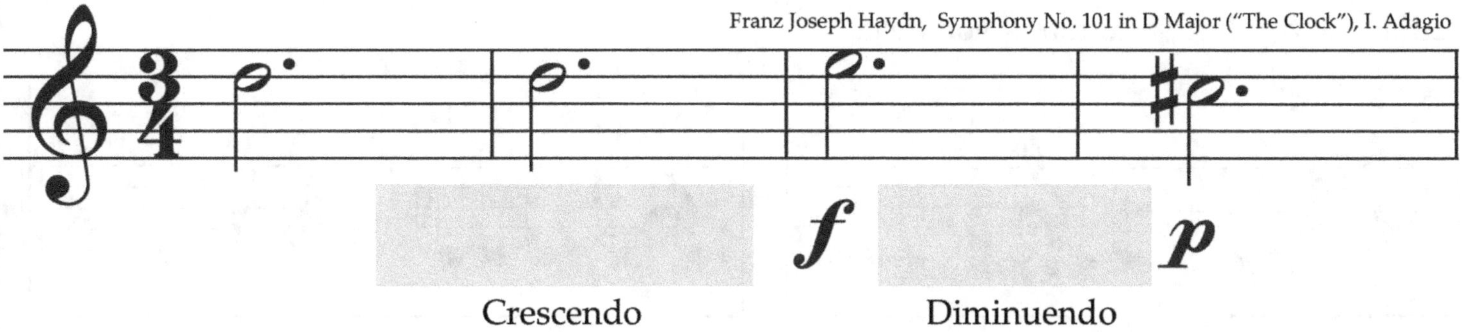

Johann Sebastian Bach, Suite in G Minor, Gavotte en Rondeau, BWV 822

*f*          *mp*

Crescendo          Diminuendo

Franz Joseph Haydn,  Symphony No. 101 in D Major ("The Clock"), I. Adagio

*f*          *p*

Crescendo          Diminuendo

Peter Ilyich Tchaikovsky, Serenade for Strings, II. Valtz

*p*

Crescendo          Diminuendo

4. Draw the clef. Write the other name for each clef on the line.

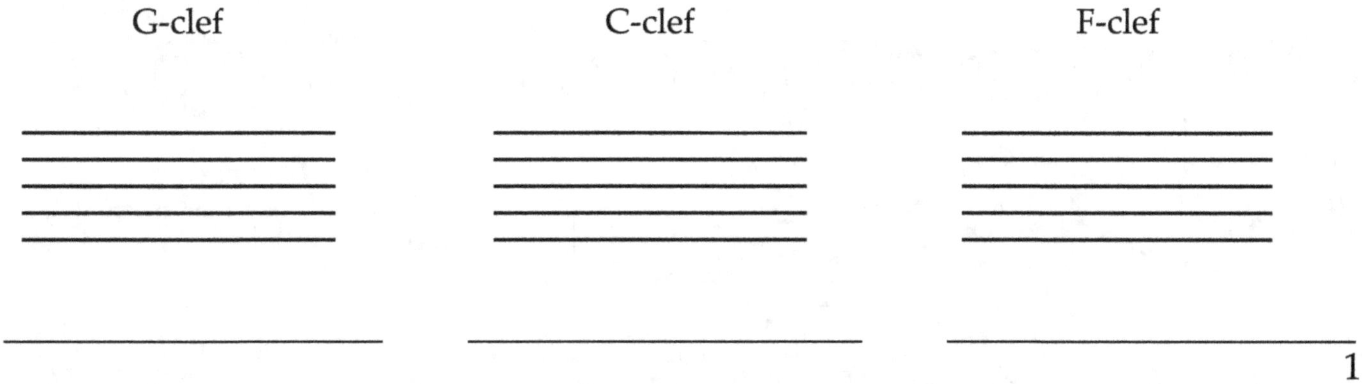

G-clef          C-clef          F-clef

_____          _____          _____

# What do you hear? #3

Circle the dynamic you hear. You will hear a crescendo, a diminuendo or both.

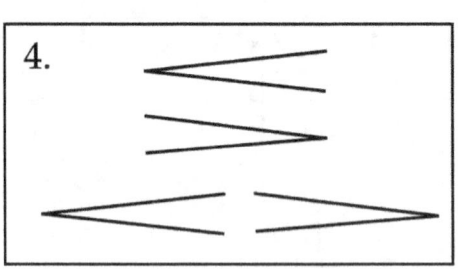

1.

Crescendo

Diminuendo

Both

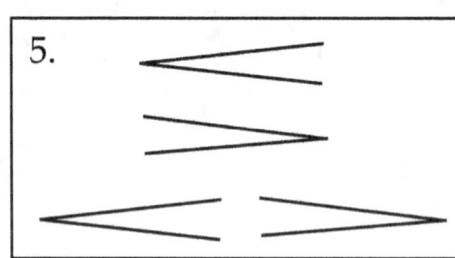

2.

Crescendo

Diminuendo

Both

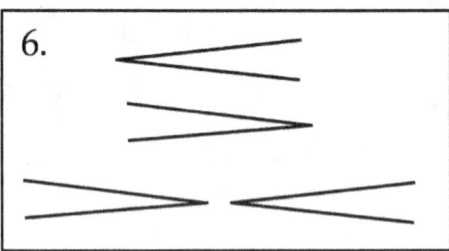

3.

Crescendo

Diminuendo

Both

4.

5.

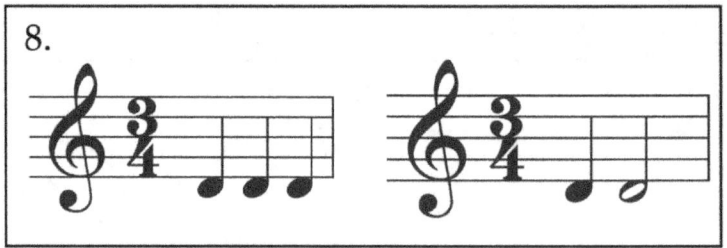

6.

*\* Additional dynamics exercise found on p. 100*

Circle the rhythm pattern that you hear.

7.

8.

*\* Additional rhythm ID exercise found on p. 101*

Choose from these examples for questions 1 – 6.

Ludwig van Beethoven, Sonata No. 5 in F Major, Op. 24, I. Allegro

Sergei Rachmaninoff, Vocalise

Gabriel Fauré, Pavane, Op. 50

Johann Sebastian Bach, Brandenburg Concerto No. 5, I. Allegro

Max Reger, Suite No. 1 in G Minor for Solo Viola, Op. 131

Wolfgang Amadeus Mozart, Symphony No. 40, IV. Allegro assai

Sergei Rachmaninoff, Cello Sonata, Op. 19, I. Lento

Choose a rhythm pattern for questions 7-8 from each box.

# Lesson 5

**Rhythm** is how long or short we hold notes. Rhythm is measured and counted in beats. Each note and rest receives a specific number of beats.

| Name | Symbol | Rest | Beats |
|------|--------|------|-------|
| Quarter Note | ♩ | 𝄽 | 1 |
| Half Note | ♩ | ▬ | 2 |
| Dotted Half Note | ♩. | | 3 |
| Whole Note | o | ▬ | 4 (or rest a whole measure) |

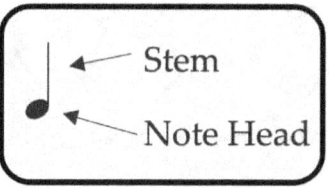

Stem
Note Head

Remember that handwritten music should not look like the computer font. You don't need to color the sides of the notes.

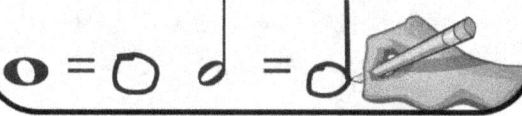

Don't forget! Count the staff lines up from bottom to top.

## Stem Rules

- ☐ If the note is BELOW staff line 3, the stem goes UP on the right.
- ☐ If the note is ABOVE staff line 3, the stem goes DOWN on the left.
- ☐ If the note is on line 3, the stem can go UP or DOWN.
- ☐ Draw the stem through 3 lines or 3 spaces.

1. Draw a treble clef. Then, make each note head a quarter note.

2. Trace the rest. Then draw rest in the empty measure.

A quarter rest is drawn between lines 2 and 4.

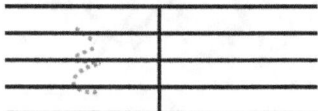

The half rest sits on line 3

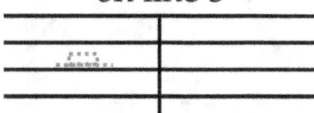

The whole rest dangles from line 4.

Number of Beats _____          Number of Beats _____          Number of Beats _____

3. Draw the note in the box.

Quarter Note          Half Note          Dotted Half Note          Whole Note

4. Write the number of beats each note or rest gets in the hearts.

5. **Bar lines** create **measures.** How many measures are in the example above? _____

6. A **double bar line** shows the end of the piece of music. Circle the double bar line.

The **time signature** is written on the right side of the clef at the beginning of a piece. The top number tells us how many beats are in each measure. The bottom number tells us what kind of note gets one beat. If the bottom number is a 4, *it means a quarter note gets 1 beat.*

7. Circle the top number of each time signature. Write the number of beats for each note or rest in the hearts. Write the counts for each measure on the lines. If a note gets more than one beat draw a dash between the counting numbers.

Traditional, Go Tell Aunt Rhody

Beats:

Counts:  1 - 2    3    4    _____ _____ _____    _____ _____    _____ _____ _____

Wolfgang Amadeus Mozart, Symphony No. 39, I. Allegro

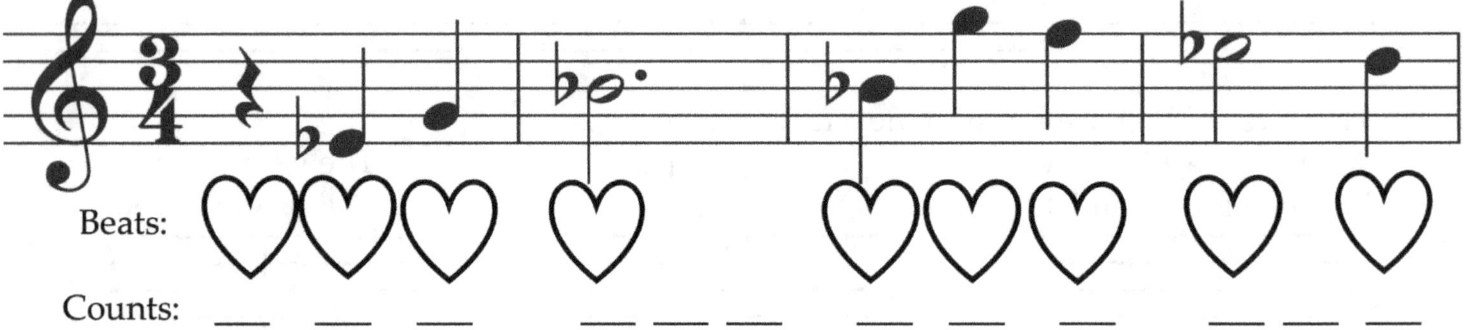

Beats:

Counts:  ___  ___  ___    ___  ___  ___    ___  ___  ___

Tomaso Antonio Vitali, Chaccone

Beats:

Counts:  ___  ___  ___    ___  ___  ___    ___  ___  ___

20

## What You Need:
- 6-sided die
- 10-20 coins

## How to Play:
Roll the die. Using the chart at the bottom, match the number to the letter. Find a note on the bingo board that is that letter. Cover it with a coin. The game is over when you have 5 coins in a row.

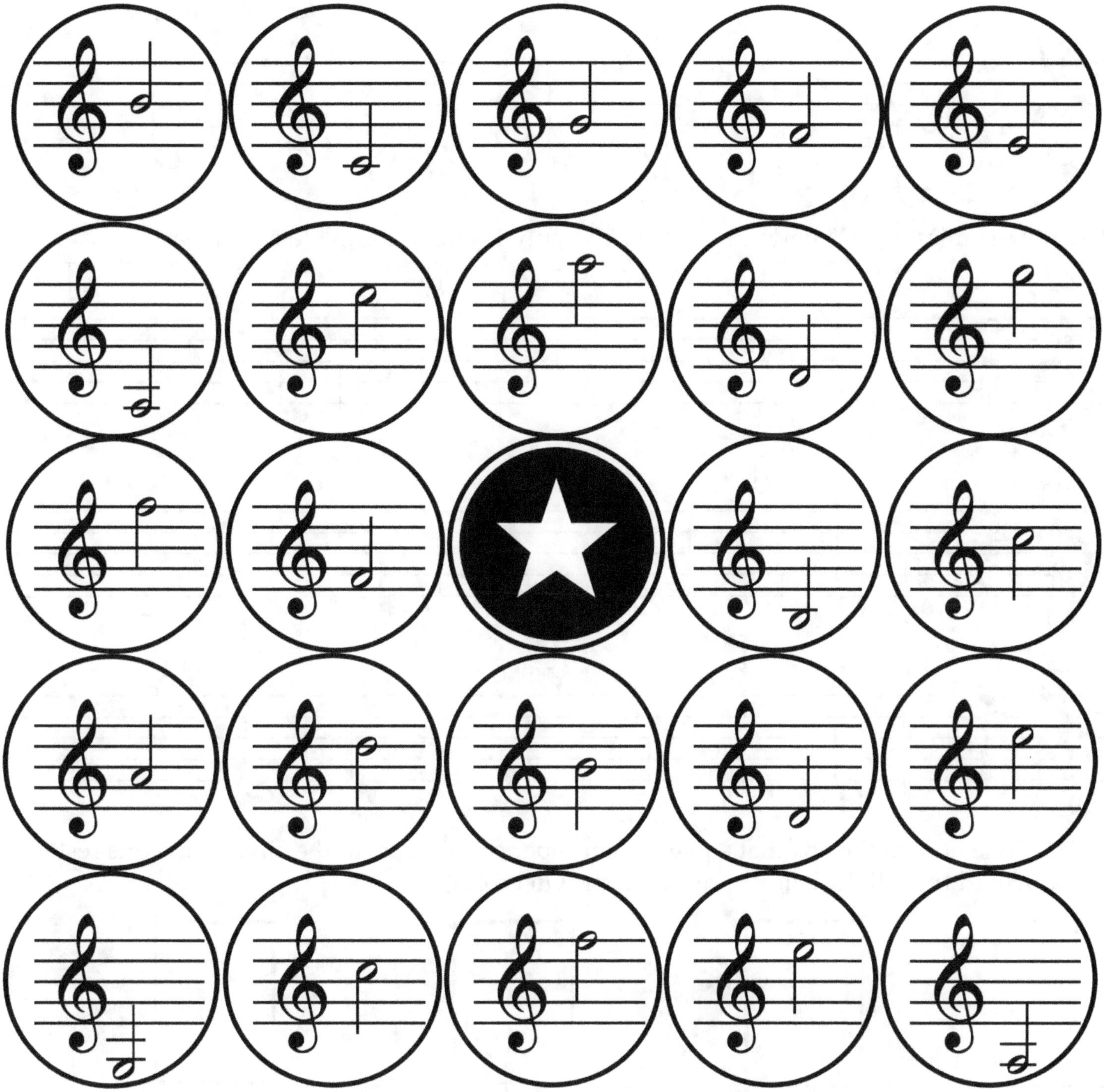

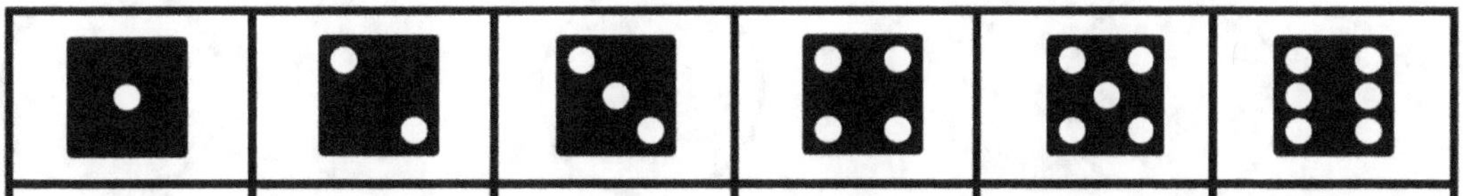

| ⚀ | ⚁ | ⚂ | ⚃ | ⚄ | ⚅ |
|---|---|---|---|---|---|
| A | B | C | D | E | F |

# Lesson 6

1. Draw the missing bar lines and the double bar line at the end of each line.

Johann Strauss II, The Blue Danube Waltz

Gustav Holst, The Planets: Mars

2. Draw the missing "D" under the arrow. Use only 1 note to complete each measure.

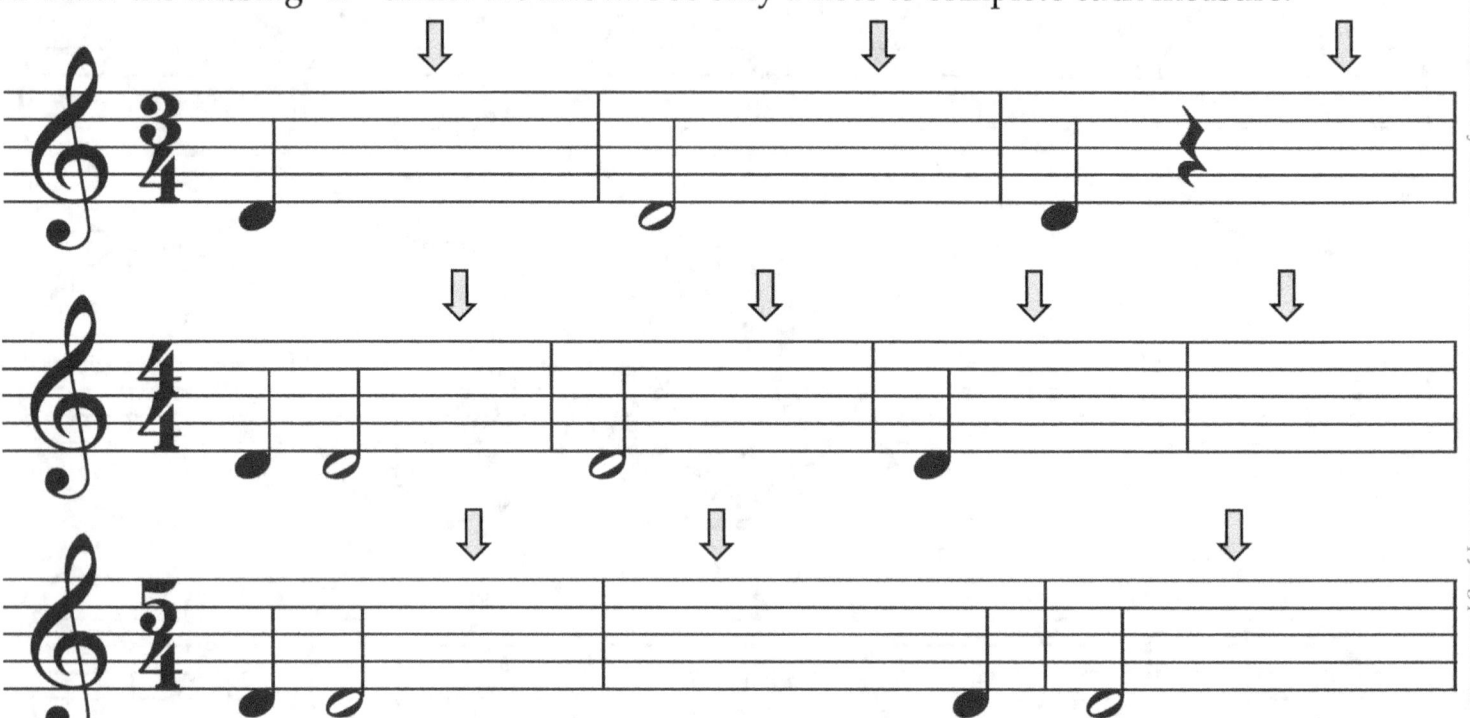

3. Draw one note in the box that equals the number of balloons. In the circle draw one rest that would pop all the balloons. (One circle will be empty.)

4. Write the number of beats for each note or rest in the hearts. Write the counts on the lines.

Jean Sibelius, Finlandia

Beats:

Counts:  ___   ___   ___   ___   ___   ___   ___   ___ ___ ___

A **repeat sign** is a double bar line with 2 dots on either side of line 3. When the thin line and the dots are on the right side of the thick line, it is called a **forward repeat.** This means that you repeat the music that is in between the two repeat signs.

Johann Sebastian Bach, Minuet

5. Draw a repeat sign at the end of measure 3. Then draw a forward repeat sign at the beginning of measure 2.

**Da Capo al Fine** or **D.C. al Fine** is an Italian term that means repeat. In Italian **Da Capo** [da ca-poh] means "the head." The head of a piece is the beginning. Instead of writing out Da Capo, composers will abbreviate it D. C. In Italian the word **Fine** [fee-neh] means "finish." So, **D.C. al Fine** means "go back to the beginning and play up to where "Fine" is printed.

6. What piece have you played that has a D.C. al Fine? _____

7. Draw the missing REST under each arrow. Only use one rest to complete each measure.

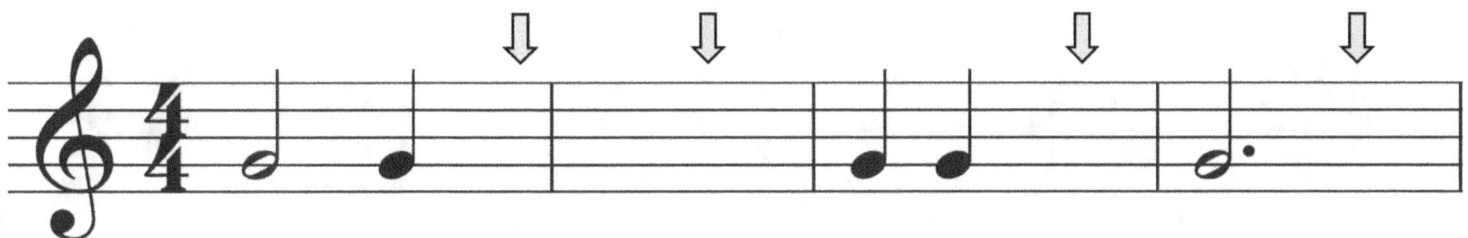

# Lesson 7

1. Write the top number of the time signature on each tortilla chip to know which salsa bowl it goes in.

The Magic of Music Theory Book 2 - © 2025 Horsehair Music. Photocopying prohibited.

## Discover the Composers

Fill in the letters of the notes to learn about the life of a great composer while you listen to Serenade for Strings, IV. Larghetto, by Antonin Dvořák. [An-toe-nin Duh-vor-shjock]

___ntonin ___vořák was ___orn in the ___zech R___pu___li___ in 1841 to

a villa___e ___ut___her. He l___ ___rned to play the violin, viol___, or___ ___n,

and pi___no and loved to play ___or villa___e dan___ ___s. ___voř___k

be___an ___omposing ___t 23 years old. He inclu___ ___ ___ ___olk tunes

in his musi___. He ___ame to N___w York in 1892 to te___ch ___omposition.

While in ___meri___ ___ he wrote his 9th symphony, "The N___w Worl___."

25

# Lesson 8

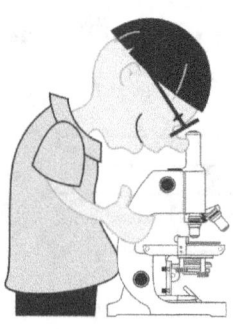

Jack and Candace stayed after school to work on their science lab. Since Jack is always very hungry after school, his mom packed him an extra snack. Jack got out his bag of snacks while Candace was getting out the microscope. Candace said, "Aw, rats! I wish I had thought to ask my mom to pack a snack today. I'm starving. Lunch feels like it was forever ago." Jack looked over and said, "Hey, my mom packed enough that I can share with you." So, Candace opened her empty lunch bag. Jack took the cookie and broke it in half. He kept half and put half on Candace's bag. Then he got out the banana. He peeled it and let Candace break off half. Then he took the blueberry muffin and split that in half and gave half to Candace. Jack looked up, "Hey, do you remember Mr. Jones was talking about how 1 flatworm can split in half and regrow?" Candace made a face and said, "Eww, yes. I thought that was disgusting!" Suddenly a voice came over the intercom, "Candace Lee, please come to the office." Candace looked over at Jack, "Oh no! I forgot I have a cello lesson today! Do you want your half of the snacks back?" "No, that's ok. Take your half with you and you can eat it in in the car," Jack said. "Ok. Thanks, Jack!" Candace began to pack up her book and lunch bag. "I'll see you tomorrow. Can you put the microscope away when you're done?" Jack looked up. "Sure. No problem. Have a good cello lesson!"

Jack worked on his worksheet as he ate his half of the cookie. It wasn't nearly as fun to do science lab by yourself. He felt a little droopy now because there was no one to talk to and work with. He finished the worksheet, put the microscope away and packed up. He couldn't be late for his violin lesson. His teacher said they were going to learn about eighth notes today.

At his violin lesson that day Jack learned that 1 quarter note can be split in half into 2 eighth notes. It made him think about splitting his snack with Candace earlier that day. He started with 1 banana. After he split it, he still had 1 banana, but it was in 2 pieces – 2 halves.

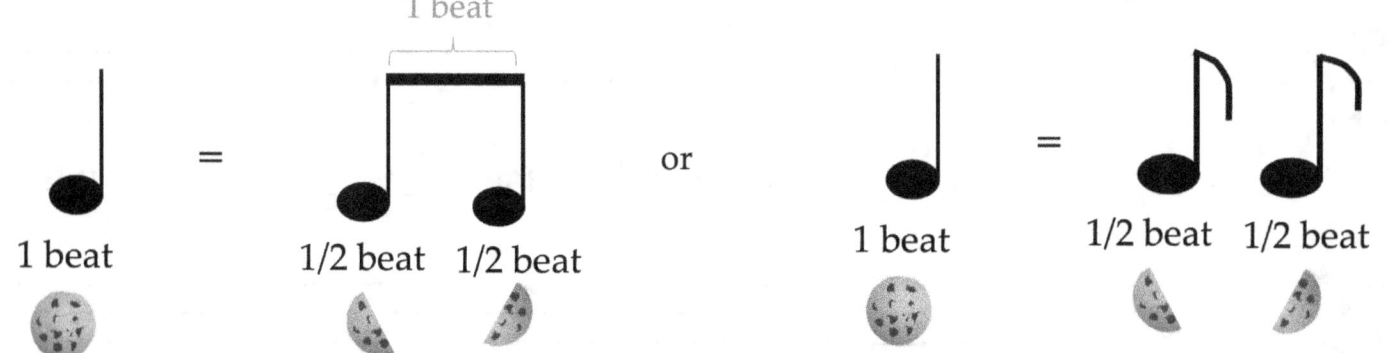

When Candace was there it was like the beamed eighth notes. They were working together, and they each got half of the snack. He remembered he felt droopy when Candace left and he was alone with his half of the snacks. The eighth note with the flag looked droopy just like he felt.

2 eighth notes are joined together by a **beam**.          1 eighth note alone has a **flag**.

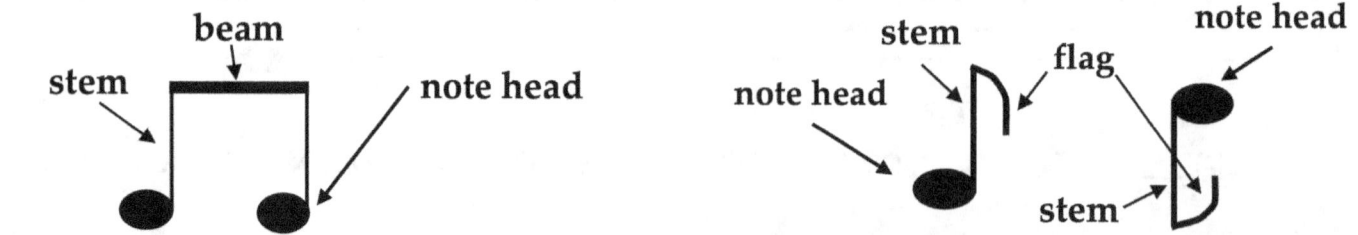

The Magic of Music Theory Book 2 - © 2023 Horsehair Music. Photocopying prohibited.

3. Trace the eighth notes and color in the note heads.

We count eighth notes by saying "1, and, 2, and, 3, and, 4, and," When writing the counts for eighth notes, write the number under the first eighth note. Then write a "+" under the second eighth note to show the second half of the beat. When you see the "+" you will say "and."

Beats:  ½  ½  ½  ½  ½  ½  ½  ½  ½  ½  1  ½  ½  1

Counts:  1  +  2  +  3  +  4  +  1  +  2  +  3  +  4  +

2. Write the number of beats for each note in the hearts. Then, write the counts on the lines.

Alexander Borodin, Prince Igor

Beats:

Counts:  ___  ___  ___  ___  ___  ___  ___  ___  ___

Christian Petzold, Minuet in G Major

Beats:

Counts:  ___  ___  ___  ___  ___  ___  ___  ___  ___  ___

Johann Sebastian Bach, Musette, BWV 126

Beats:

Counts:  ___  ___  ___  ___  ___  ___  ___  ___  ___  ___

# What do you hear? #4

Draw the symbol for a crescendo or diminuendo that you hear in each box.

| | | |
|---|---|---|
| 1. | 2. | 3. |

*\* Additional dynamics exercise found on p. 100*

Circle the rhythm pattern you hear.

*\* Additional rhythm ID exercise found on p. 101*

**Rhythm Writing:**

You will hear a rhythm pattern on open D. The teacher will count 1 measure so that you know the tempo. (This is called a "measure for free.") You will hear quarter notes or half notes. In the boxes below, draw all the notes you hear in the order that you hear them.

6. 𝄴

7. 𝄴

*\* Additional rhythm writing exercise found on p. 104*

Choose from these examples for questions 1 – 3.

Friedrich Seitz, Concerto No. 2 in G Major, Op. 13, III. Allegretto moderato

Luigi Boccherini, Minuet

Pablo de Sarasate, Introduction & Tarantella

*dim.*

*cresc.*

*dim.*

Choose one example in each box for questions 4 & 5.

Choose from these examples for questions 6 & 7 or create your own example.

# Lesson 9

To draw eighth notes on the staff, draw two quarter notes. Then draw a horizontal line connecting the ends of the stems.

1. Trace the dotted lines and color in the note heads to draw eighth notes.

**Eighth Note Stem and Beam Rules:**
- ❏ If both notes are below line 3, the stems go up on the right.
- ❏ If both notes are on or above line 3, the stems go down on the left.
- ❏ If one stem should go up and the other stem should go down. Then use the stem rule for the note farthest from line 3 for both notes.
- ❏ Connect the top of the stems with a horizonal or slanted line.

2. Draw a treble clef. Trace these eighth notes that are different pitches.

3. Draw a treble clef. Then circle the note in each set of eighth notes that is farthest from line 3.

4. Draw a treble clef. Trace line 3 with a colored pencil. For each pair of eighth notes, circle the note that is farthest from line 3. Then, trace the eighth notes and color in the note heads.

5. Draw a treble clef. Draw stems and beams for each set of eighth notes.

6. Write the beats for each note in the hearts. Write the counts on the line.

Wolfgang Amadeus Mozart, German Dance No. 3, K. 605

Beats:

Counts: _ _ _ _ _ _ _ _ _ _ _ _ _ _

Ludwig van Beethoven, Cello Sonata No. 3, Op. 69, I. Allegro, ma non tanto

Beats:

Counts: _ _ _ _ _ _ _ _ _ _ _ _ _ _ _ _ _ _ _

7. Fill in the top number of the time signature for each measure.

8. Draw the missing bar lines and a double bar line at the end.

Thomas Bayle, Long Long Ago

Jean Gabriel-Marie, La Cinquantaine

30

# Lesson 10

Since two eighth notes share 1 beat, one eighth note alone gets ½ of a beat. Single eighth notes use the same stem rules as quarter notes. (p. 19) It does not matter if the stem is going up or down, the flag *always* points to the right.

1. Trace the dotted lines and color in the note heads to create eighth notes with flags. Write the number of beats each note gets in the hearts.

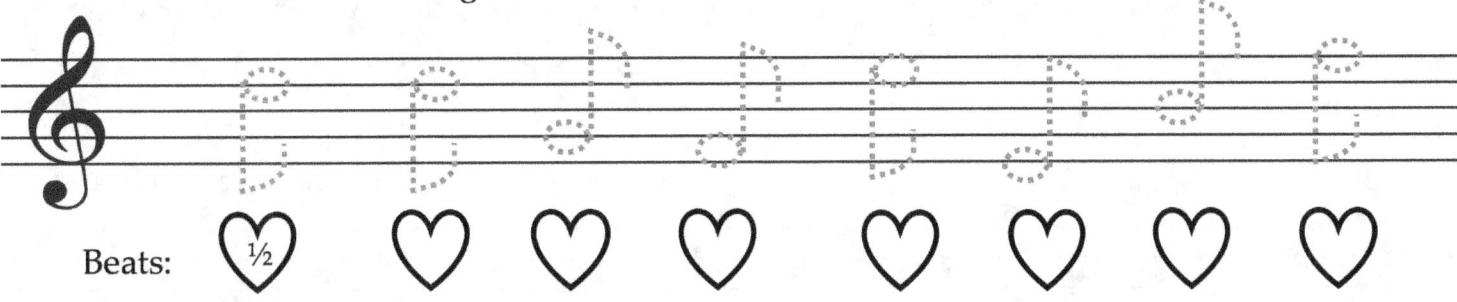

Beats: ½

2. Draw an eighth note with a flag on the staff that matches the letter below.

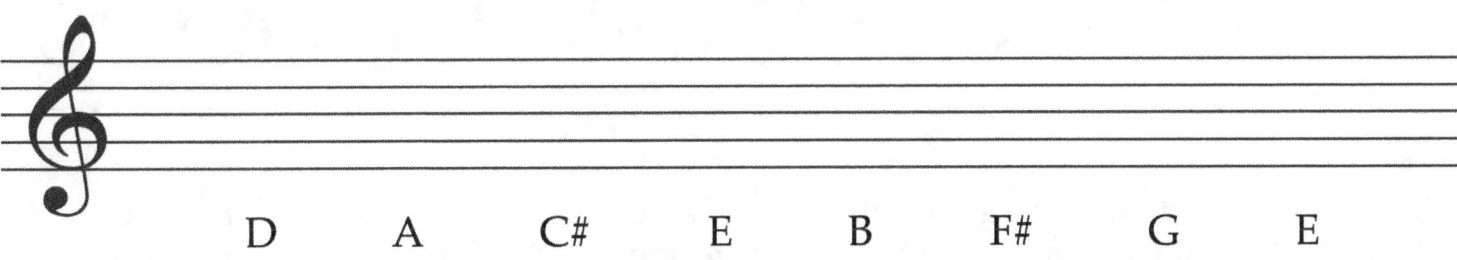

D     A     C#     E     B     F#     G     E

An **eighth rest** looks like the number 7 with a dot on it. To draw an eighth rest, draw a little dot in space 3. Then draw a "7" that ends on line 2.

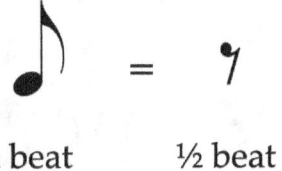

½ beat     ½ beat

3. Trace the eighth rests.

½     ½

4. Draw a treble clef. Draw 4 more eighth rests on the staff.

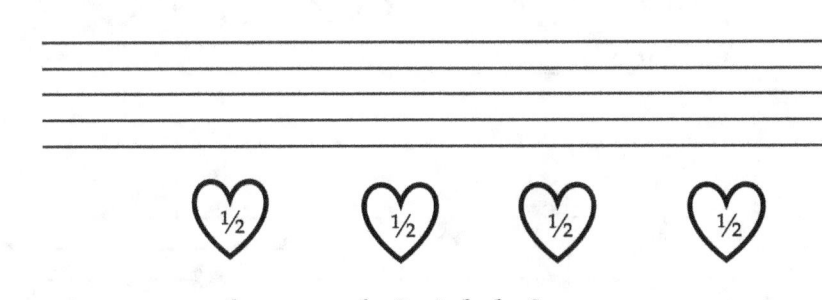

½     ½     ½     ½

5. How would you draw a rest or rests that equals 2 eighths?

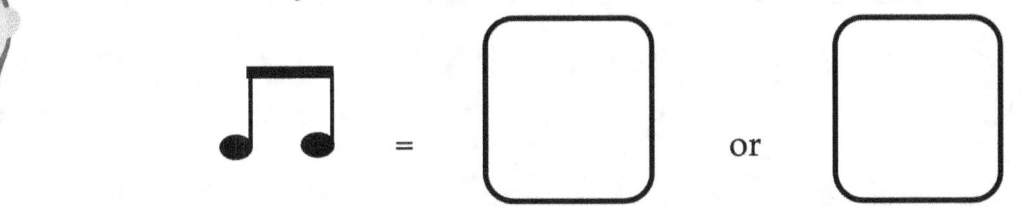

=          or

31

6. Write the beats for each note or rest in the hearts. Then write the counts on the lines.

Max Bruch, Kol Nidrei, Hebrew Melody

Beats:

Counts:

Antonio Vivaldi, Concerto in F Major, Op. 8, No. 3 "Autumn," I. Allegro

Beats:

Counts:

Beats are grouped into 2 categories: **strong** and **weak**. Numbered beats are strong beats. The "and" of the beat is a weak beats. Weak beats are also called **off-beats**. When off-beats or weak beats are emphasized, it is called **syncopation**.

syncopation

Franz Schubert, String Quartet No. 13 in A Minor, Op. 29, II. Andante

Beats:

Counts:

Antonin Dvořák, Sonatina, Op. 100, I. Allegro risoluto

Beats:

Counts:

# Lesson 11

**Ragtime** is a type of American music. It was born in the southern region of the United States in the early 1920s. Ragtime combined elements from classical music, jazz, African-American folk tunes, and spirituals. One of the main characteristics of ragtime is **syncopation**. It emphasizes the off-beat. On the next page, you will learn more about Scott Joplin who was one of the greatest composers of ragtime.

1. Write in the counting. Circle the syncopation.

Scott Joplin, The Entertainer

Beats:

Counts: ___ ___   ___ ___   ___ ___   ___ ___ ___   ___ ___ ___   ___ ___

2. Circle the rests hidden in the reef with the manatees. There are 3 quarter rests, 3 eighth rests, 1 half rest and 2 whole rests.

*Discover the Composers*

Fill in the letters of the notes to learn about the life of a great composer while you listen to The Entertainer, by Scott Joplin.

S___ott Joplin was ___orn into a musi___al ___amily in T___x___rk___na, Arkansas.

His mom sang and pl___yed the ___ ___njo and his ___ather pl___y___ ___ the violin.

Joplin t___u___ht himsel___ to play the piano. He ___ ___ ___ ___n to compose

in a new style o___ music ___ all___ ___ Ra___time. Ragtime ___om___ine ___

rhythms and harmonies from ___ ___ri___ ___n-Am___ri___an music and classical

music. Over one million ___opies w___re sol___ of his composition, M___ple

L___ ___ ___ Ra___. Joplin is ___ ___ll___ ___ "The King of R___ ___time."

4. What instrument(s) did you hear?_____

5. Did you hear any syncopation?_____

34

The Magic of Music Theory Book 2 – © 2023 Horsehair Music. Photocopying prohibited.

# Lesson 12

**Tempo** means speed. Music uses Italian words to tell the tempo of a piece.

**Largo** – very slow
**Adagio** – slow
**Andante** – walking speed
**Allegro** – fast, happy, with energy
**Presto** – very fast
**Prestissimo** [press-tee-see-mo] – very, very fast

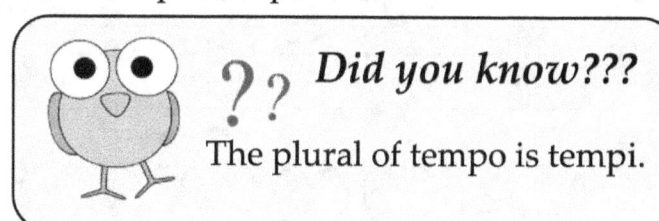

**?? *Did you know???***
The plural of tempo is tempi.

*Ritardando* [rih-tar-dahn-dough] means to gradually slow down. Sometimes you will just see a shortened form of the word, *ritard.* [rih-tard]. And sometimes you will see just the first 3 letters *rit.* They all mean the same thing, slow down!

After a ritard, if the composer wants you to return to the original tempo you were playing, you will see *a tempo* [ah tehm-po].

1. Write the Italian word next to the speed limit sign that would match the speed limit sign or road sign.

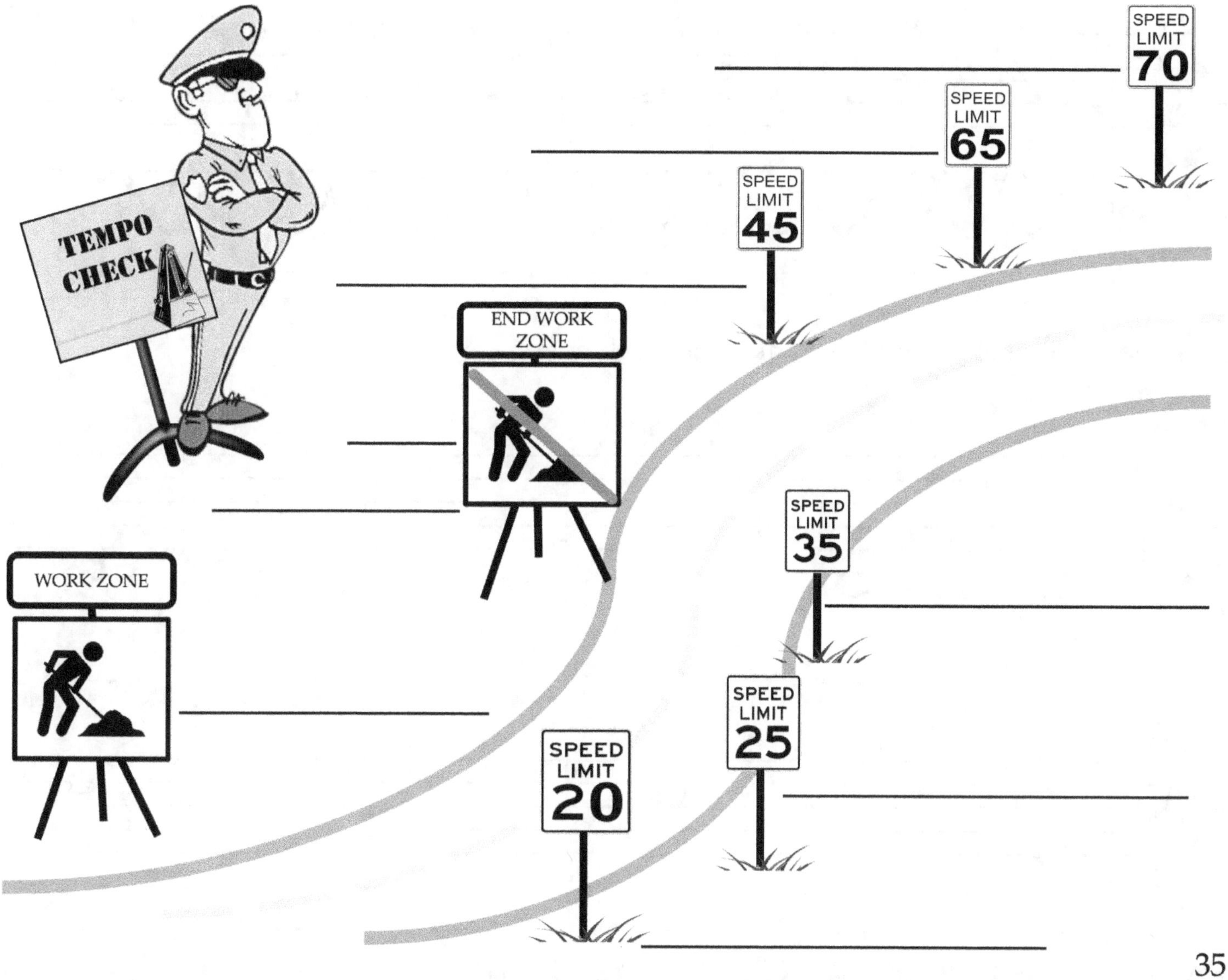

2. Write the beats for each note in the hearts and write the counts on the lines.

Carl Bohm, Sarabande

Beats:

Counts: _ _ _ _ _ _ _ _ _ _ _

Alfred Moffat, Berceuse

Beats:

Counts: _ _ _ _ _ _ _ _

Edward Mollenhauer, Fantasia, The Boy Paganini

Beats:

Counts: _ _ _ _ _ _ _ _ _ _ _ _ _ _ _

3. Write the letter name on the blank under each note.

_ _ _ _ _ _

_ _ _ _ _ _

# What do you hear? #5

You will hear 3 notes. The first two are given to you. The third note will step up, step down, or repeat. Draw the note you hear as a quarter note on the correct line or space in each measure.

*\* Additional step, skip, repeat exercise found on p. 102*

**Rhythm Writing:**

You will hear a rhythm pattern on open D. You will hear 1 measure counted out loud "for free" so you will know the tempo. You will hear quarter notes, half notes, dotted half notes, or a whole note. In each box below, write the notes you hear in the order that you hear them.

4.

5.

*\* Additional rhythm writing exercise found on p. 104*

For questions 1 – 3, the teacher should play the two notes in the measure and then choose a pitch that steps up, steps down, or repeats.

For questions 4 and 5, the teacher can choose one for each box from the examples below. Play the example multiple times.

# Lesson 13

There are 2 types of steps: a **half step** and a **whole step**. A **half step** on the fingerboard is when your fingertips are close together. It is the closest two notes can be. A **whole step** is 2 half steps together. There there is a space between your fingers.

1. Draw a circle on the fingerboard that is a *half step BELOW* the house. The first one is done for you.

Half step: Fingertips are close together.

2. Draw a circle on the fingerboard that is a *whole step BELOW* the house. The first one is done for you.

Whole Step: Fingers have space between.

3. Draw a circle on the fingerboard that is *a half step ABOVE* the house.

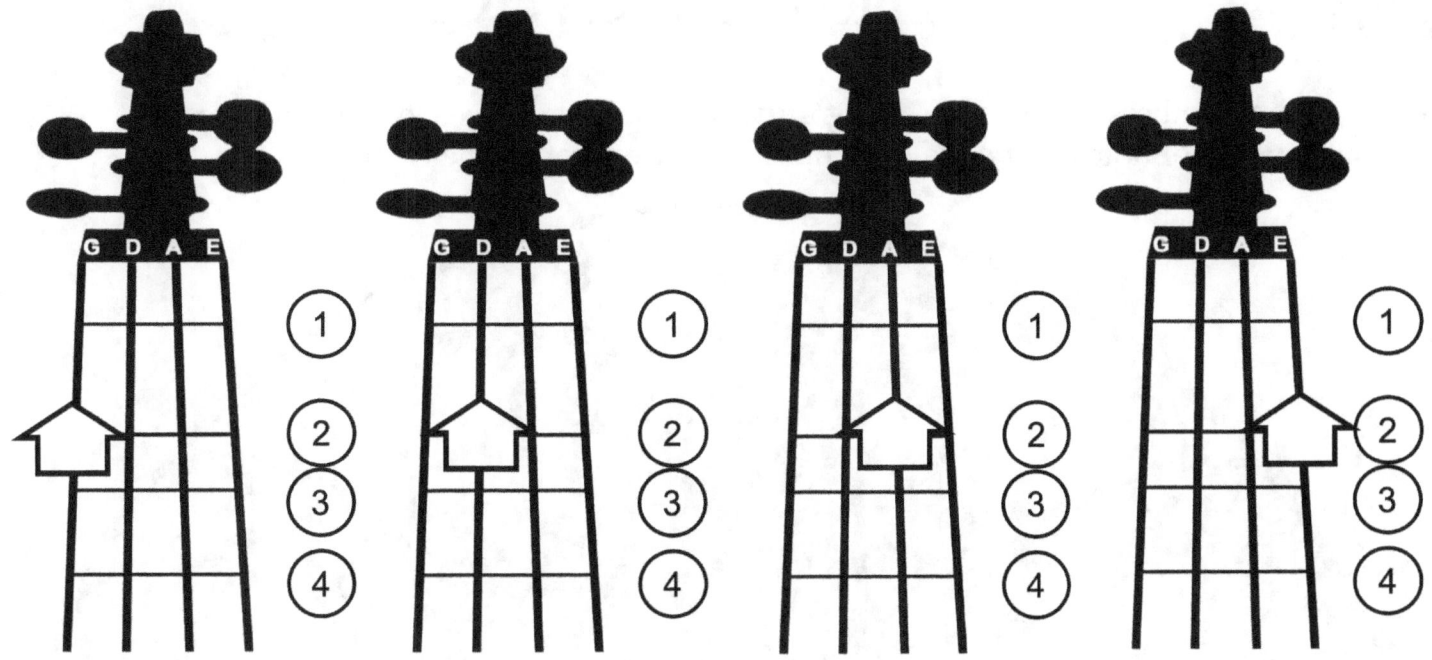

4. Draw a circle on the fingerboard that is a *whole step ABOVE* the house.

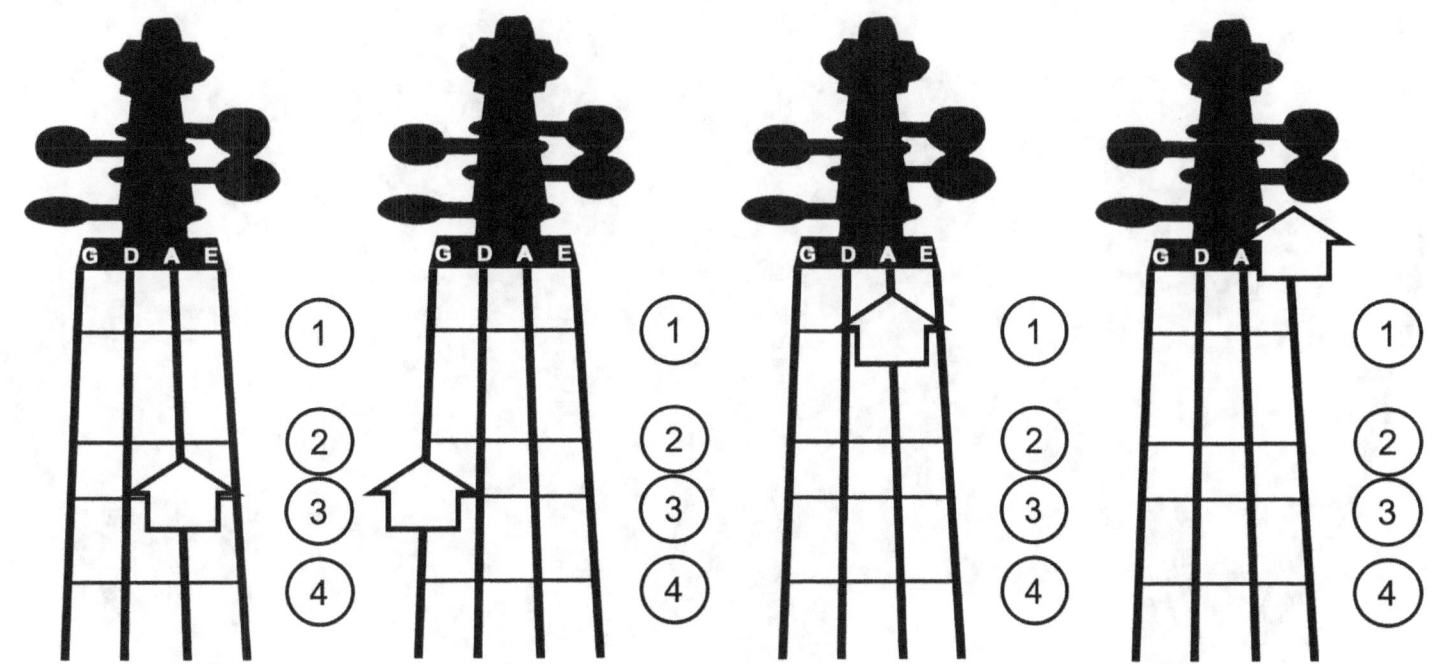

5. A _____ step is the closest distance between two fingers on the fingerboard.

6. A _____ step is when the fingers have a space between them on the fingerboard.

7. A _____ step is two _____ steps put together.

8. There is a half step between fingers _____ and _____ on the fingerboards above.

# Musical Clock

1. Write the numbers on the clock using music notes. In the boxes, draw a note or any combination of notes that equals the number placement on the clock.

2. Listen for the syncopation in The Syncopated Clock by Leroy Anderson.

3. In this piece what instrument makes the clock sound? _____

# Lesson 14

1. A half step is when our fingers are _____ together. A whole step is _____ half
   steps together. There is _____ between our fingers for a whole step.
   (number)

2. Write one letter of the music alphabet on each line starting on "A."

   _____  _____  _____  _____  _____  _____  _____

Just like you have 2 names (a first name and last name), each letter of the music alphabet has
a "last name."  It's called **natural**. When your friends talk to you, they probably don't use
your full name, but we all know that you still have a last name. If it is just the letter with no
symbol, then assume it is a natural. The natural looks like this: ♮

3. Trace the naturals:                   **How to draw a natural:**
                                          **Step 1:** Draw a capital L.     **Step 2:** Then draw a 7.

4. Draw a natural sign in the blank after each letter.

   A_____     B_____     C_____     D_____     E_____     F_____     G_____

5. Draw a treble clef. Then, trace the natural signs on the staff.

The middle "box" of the natural goes on the same space or line as the note head. On the staff
naturals are drawn on the *left* side of the note head.

6. Trace the first two naturals. Then, draw a natural by each note head.

There are 3 different **chromatic signs, sharp (♯), flat (♭), and natural (♮)**. These 3 signs move
a note by a half step. A **sharp** raises a note by 1 half step. A **flat** lowers a note by 1 half step. A
**natural** removes or cancels a sharp or flat.

A **sharp** RAISES a note by 1 half step. A sharp look like tic-tac-toe board or a hashtag.

7. Trace the sharps.

8. Draw a sharp in each box.

9. Draw a treble clef. Trace the sharps on the staff.

Sharps, like naturals, ALWAYS go on the *left* side of the note head. The "middle box" of the sharp should be on the same line or space as the note head.

10. Trace the first two sharps. Then, draw a sharp next to each note head on the staff.

11. Draw each note as a dotted half note with the chromatic sign in each measure. (Don't forget: Chromatic signs go on the left. Dots go on the right.)

| G♮ | C♯ | F♮ | E♮ | A♯ | D♮ |

| B♮ | D♯ | G♯ | A♭ | C♮ | F♯ |

12. A sharp raises a note by 1 _____ _____.

13. A _____ cancels a sharp or flat.

42

# Lesson 15

The last chromatic sign is called a **flat**. A **flat** lowers a note by 1 half step. A flat looks like a "squished b" (♭). When you have a flat tire on a bike, the bike moves *down, lower* to the ground. A flat moves a note *down, lower* by 1 half step.

1. Trace the flats.

**How to draw a flat:**
**Step 1:** Draw a line.      **Step 2:** Then draw a half of a heart.

2. Write a flat sign in the blank after each letter.

A_____  B_____  C_____  D_____  E_____  F_____  G_____

3. Draw a treble clef. Trace the flat signs on the staff.

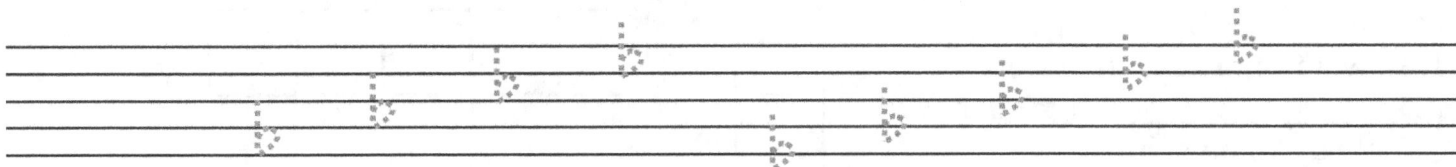

The middle of the flat goes on the same space or line as the note head. **All chromatic signs are drawn on the left side of the note head on the staff.**

4. Trace the first two flats. Then, draw a flat by each note head.

*Did you know???*
When we write a sharp or flat on the staff, it is on the *left* side of the note head. (Reading from left to right on the staff it looks like "sharp-C" or "flat-B.") When we write a sharp, flat, or natural using letters (C♯, B♭), it goes on the *right* side of the letter. It is exactly opposite! When we say the note name, we say the letter first, then the chromatic sign: "C-sharp," or "B-flat," or "G-natural."

5. Draw a whole note on the staff with the chromatic sign in each measure. (Don't forget: chromatic signs go on the left.)

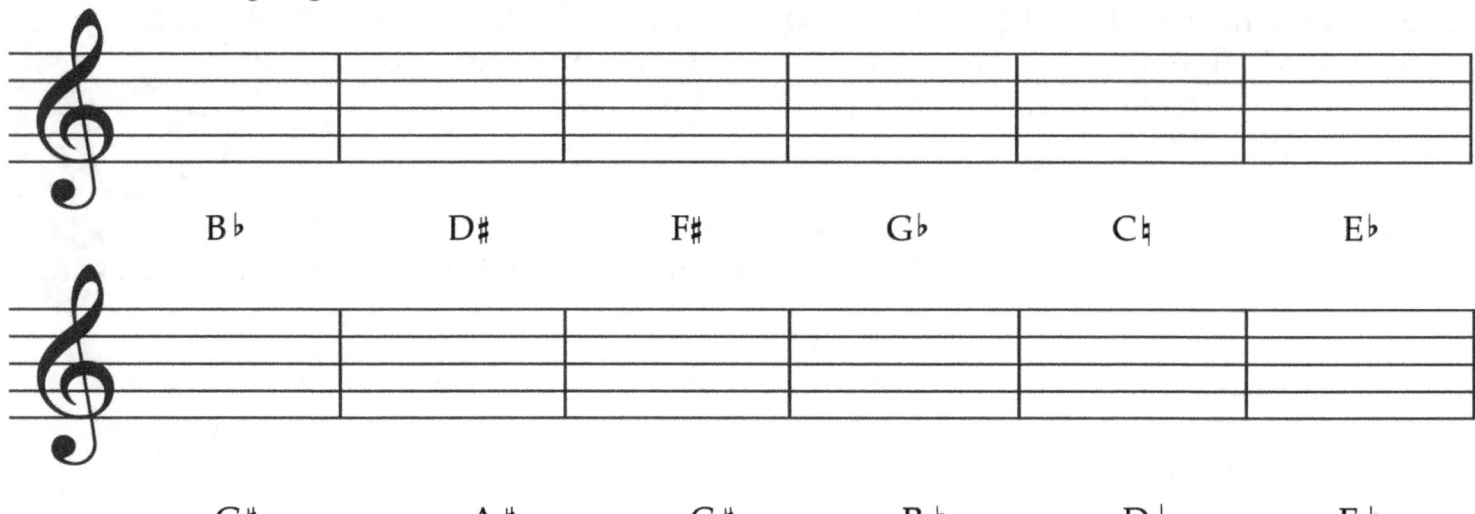

B♭          D♯          F♯          G♭          C♮          E♭

G♯          A♯          C♯          B♮          D♭          E♮

6. Fill in the terms in the crossword puzzle.

**Down**
1. Lowers a note by 1 half step.
2. A _____ sign changes a note by 1 half step.
3. Loud
4. At the beginning of each staff.

**Across**
1. Santa's helper.
2. Cancels a sharp or flat.
3. Raises a note by 1 half step
4. Sometimes called the C clef.

7. Write the letter name in the blank for each measure.

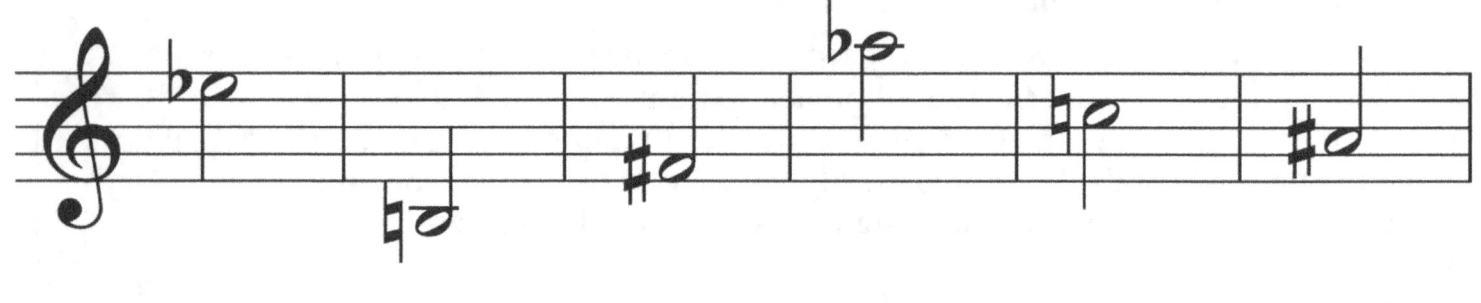

The Magic of Music Theory Book 2 - © 2025 Horsehair Music. Photocopying prohibited.

Charlie's acorns are a mess! He needs help organizing his acorns. He is keeping acorns in different trees so that he has enough for the long winter. Using the code, color the trees and the acorns the correct color.

**Color Code**
2 beats per measure = red
3 beats per measure = yellow
4 beats per measure = orange
5 beats per measure = brown

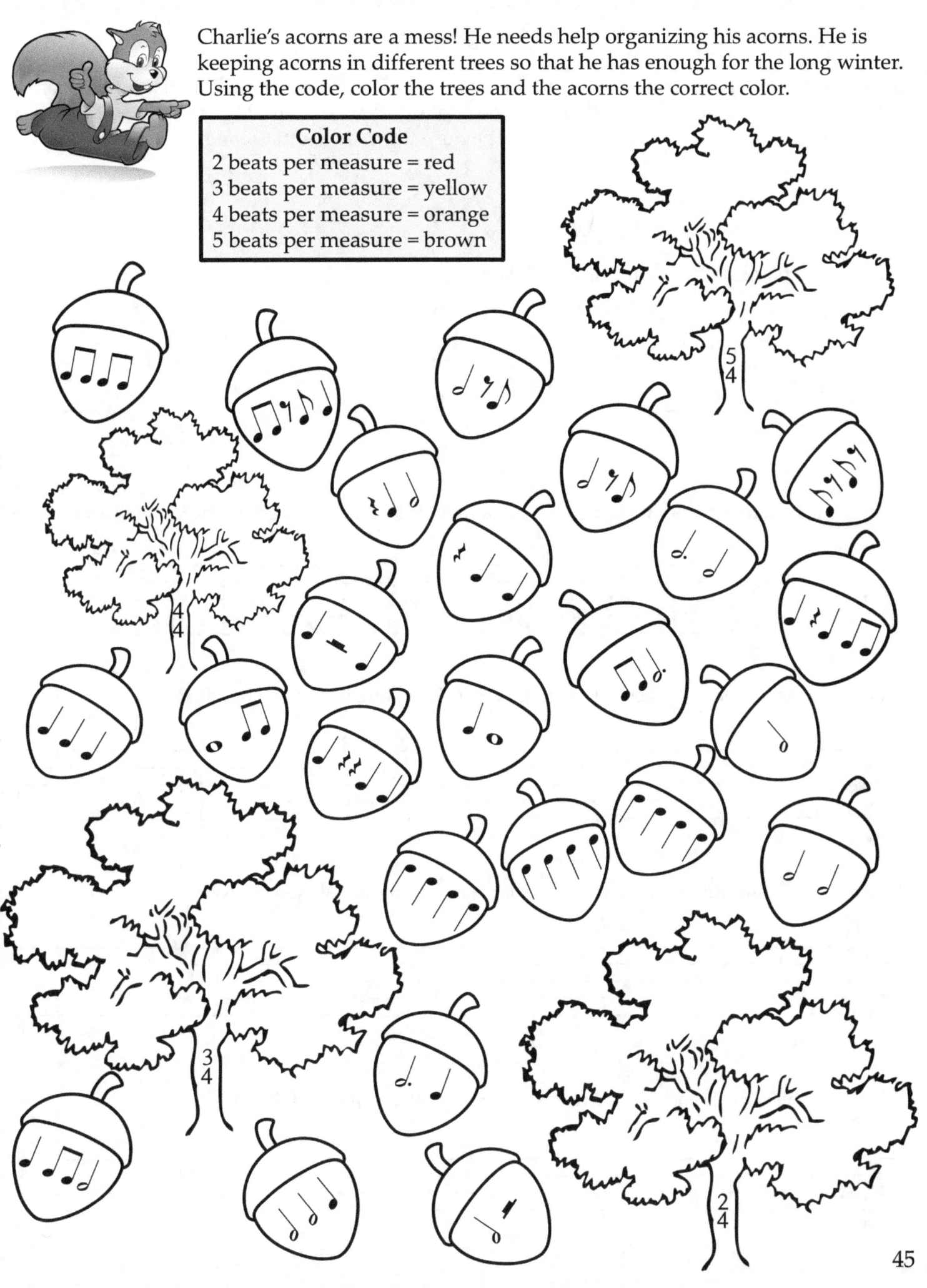

# Lesson 16

If there is not a flat or sharp next to a note, assume the letter is a natural. To raise a note from a natural by one half step, draw a sharp. To lower a note from a natural by one half step, draw a flat. These are called chromatic half steps. They use the SAME letter name.

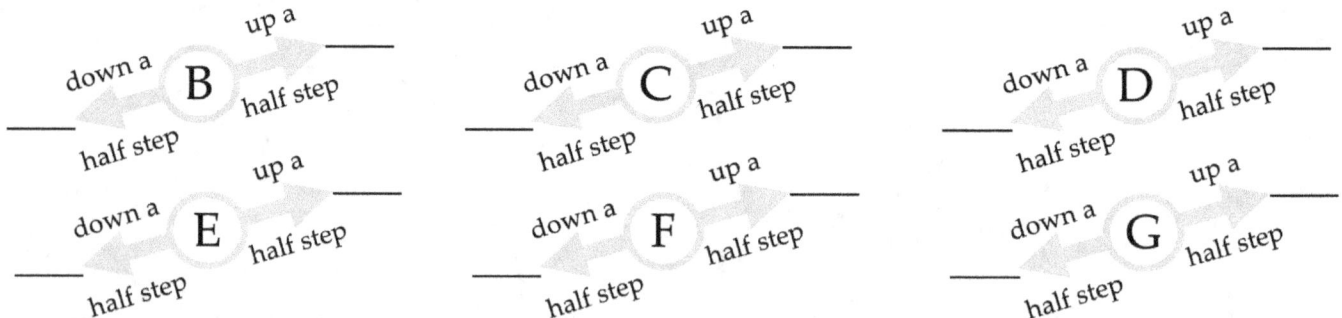

1. Fill in the blanks for the chromatic half steps

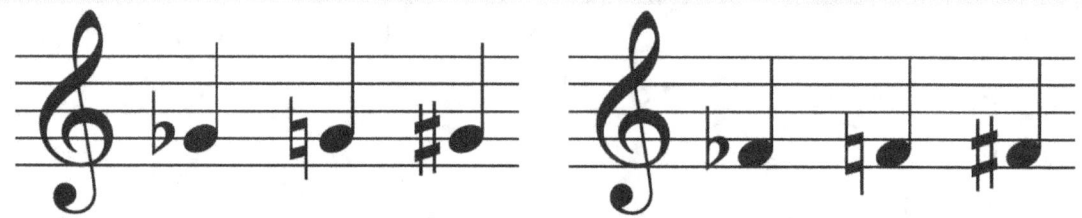

A **chromatic half step** is two notes that are a half step apart AND share the same line or space.

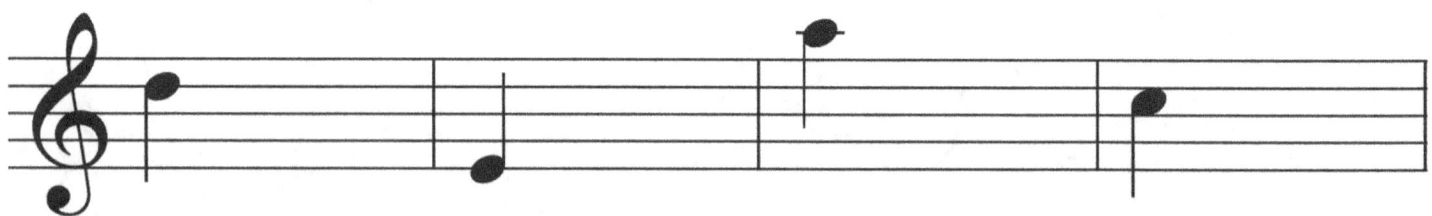

2. Draw a quarter note in each measure that is a chromatic half step HIGHER.

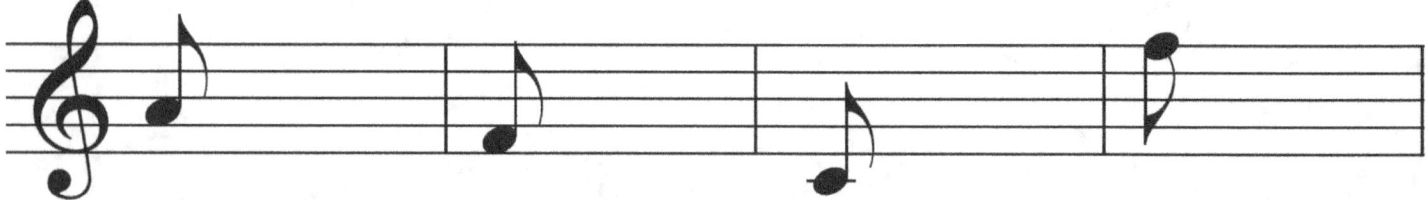

3. Draw an eighth note in each measure that is a chromatic half step LOWER.

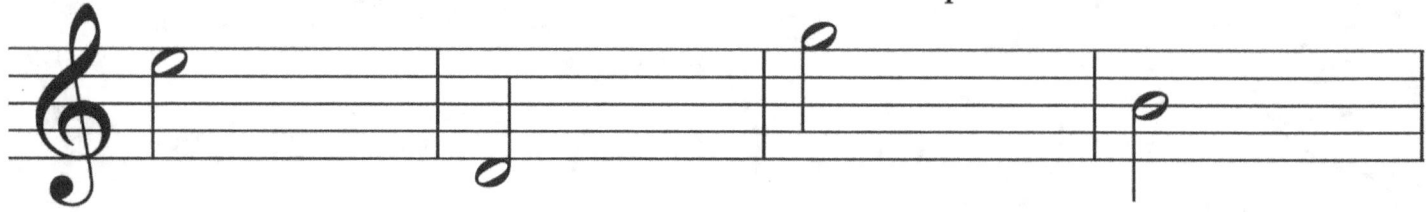

4. Draw a half note in each measure that is a chromatic half step HIGHER.

The Magic of Music Theory Book 2 - © 2023 Horsehair Music. Photocopying prohibited.

5. A _____ raises a note by 1 half step. A flat _____ a note by 1 half step.  Sharps,

flats, and naturals are called _____ signs. Two notes that are on the

same line or space and are 1 half step apart are called _____ half steps.

6. Write the letter name under each note.

Letter: ___    ___    ___    ___    ___

Letter: ___    ___    ___    ___    ___

7. Write the beats for each note in the heart and the counts on the lines.

Wolfgang Amadeus Mozart, Minuet in C Major, K. 6

Beats:

Counts: ___ ___ ___ ___    ___ ___ ___    ___    ___ ___

Ludwig van Beethoven, Concerto for Violin, I. Allegro ma non troppo

Beats:

Counts: ___ ___ ___ ___ ___    ___    ___    ___ ___ ___ ___ ___

8. Draw in the missing bar lines and double bar line.

Georg Philipp Telemann, Sonata No. 4, III. Presto

# Lesson 17

*Fingerboard Power!* A new house is going in on the A string! There is space for another house between 1st finger and 2nd finger! Since "B" up to "C♯" is a whole step, another house can fit in between them! This is "C♮," or just "C." "C" is a half step lower than "C♯." 2nd finger plays both "C" and "C♯." Because a natural cancels a sharp, it lowers the note by one half step. You will move your finger down by one half step.

1. Write the letters in each house for the A string.

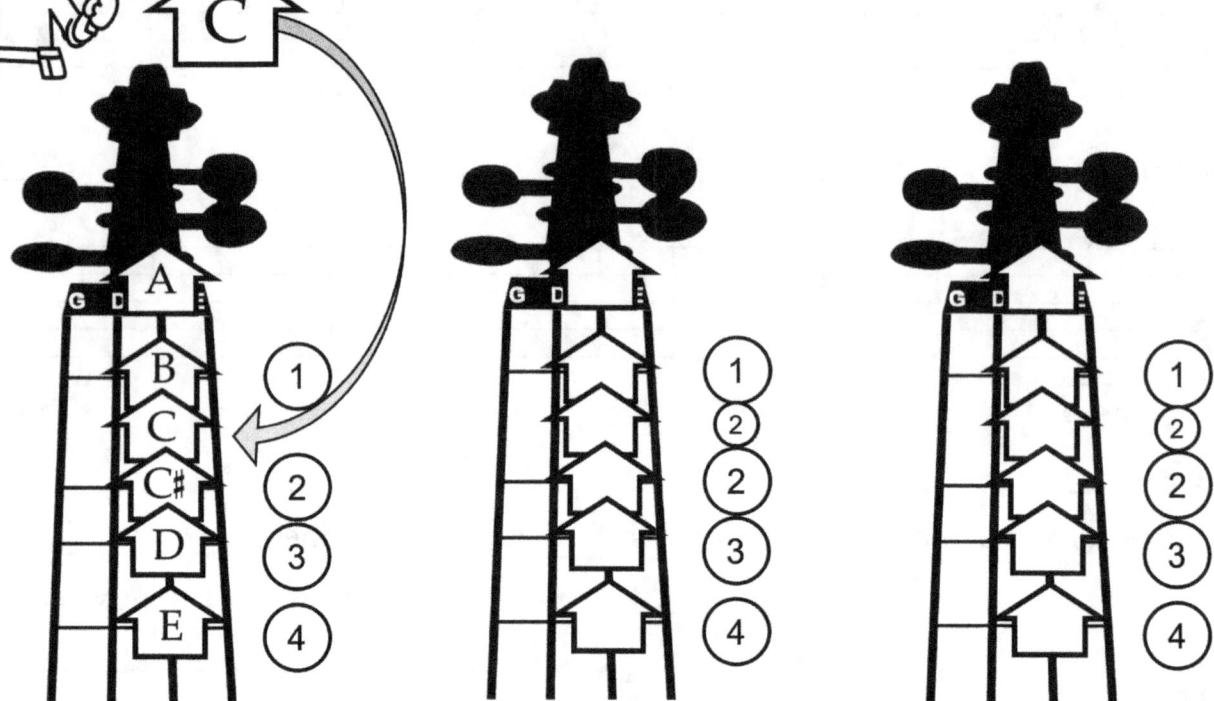

If there is a sharp by the "C" on the staff, then 2nd finger plays a half step below 3rd finger "D." If there is no sharp by the note, then 2nd finger plays a half step above 1st finger "B."

"C♮" is a chromatic half step lower than "C♯." Both "C♮" and "C♯" sit in space 4.

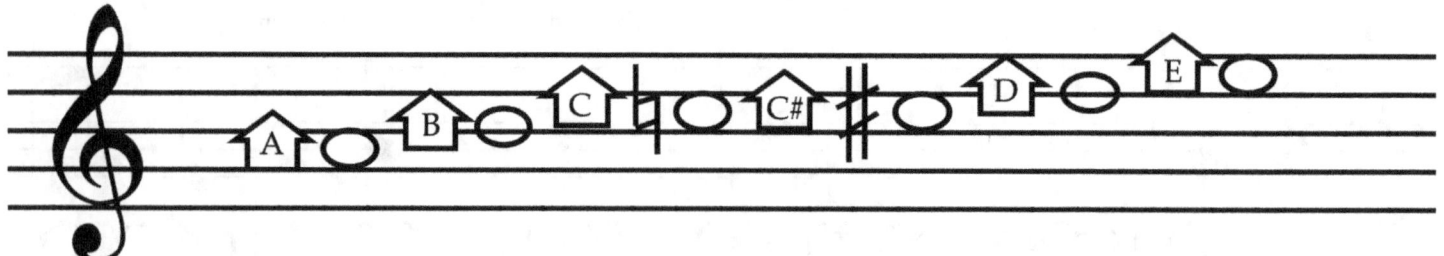

2. Draw a treble clef. Trace the "C♮" on the staff and draw 2 more. Remember to draw the natural on the left side of the note. Draw another treble clef, and trace the "C♯" on the staff and draw 2 more.

48

A new house is also on the E string between the 1st and 2nd fingers. "F#" up to "G#" is a whole step. Another house can fit between them! This is "G" or "G♮." "G" is a half step below "G#." 2nd finger plays both "G" and "G#."

3. Write the letters in each house on the E string.

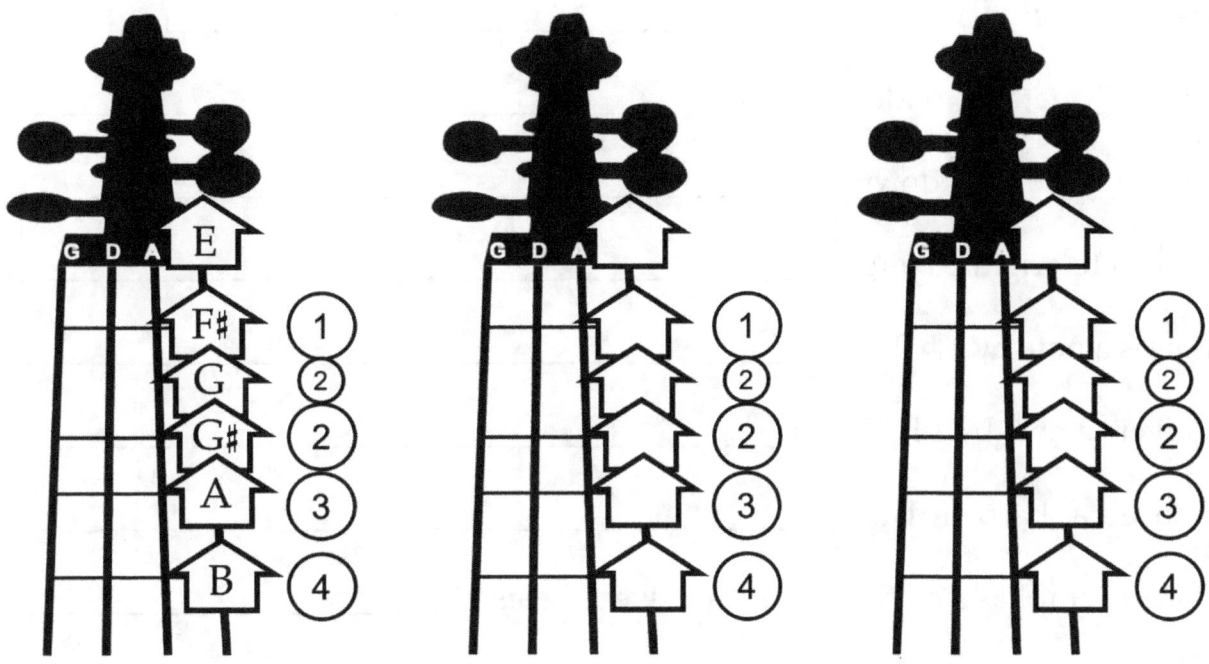

If there is a sharp by the "G" on the staff, then 2nd finger plays a half step below 3rd finger "A." If there is no sharp by the note then 2nd finger plays a half step above 1st finger "F#." Sometimes we call this "low 2."

"G" is a chromatic half step lower than "G#." Both "G♮" and "G#" sit on top of the staff.

4. Draw a treble clef. Trace the "G♮" on the staff and draw 2 more. Remember to draw the natural on the left side of the note. Draw another treble clef and trace the "G#" on the staff and draw 2 more "G-sharps."

# Fill in the terms. Then find the term in the word search.

5. Go back to the beginning and play to the finish. _____

6. A symbol that means play it again. _____

7. Gradually getting softer. _____

8. Gradually getting louder. _____

9. Gradually slowing down. _____

10. Return to original tempo. _____

11. Raises a note by 1 half step. _____

12. Lowers a note by 1 half step. _____

13. Cancels a sharp or flat. _____

14. Placing emphasis on the off-beats or weak beats. _____

**A tempo, Crescendo, D C al Fine, Diminuendo, Flat, Natural, Repeat, Ritardando, Sharp, Syncopation,**

| S | E | R | I | T | A | R | D | A | N | D | O | W |
|---|---|---|---|---|---|---|---|---|---|---|---|---|
| C | R | E | S | C | E | N | D | O | O | B | Y | X |
| G | C | H | J | M | F | Q | U | A | R | T | E | R |
| O | R | C | H | E | S | T | R | A | I | B | A | R |
| V | U | O | P | O | P | F | U | B | F | U | T | V |
| L | M | B | D | Z | Y | L | O | A | B | V | E | M |
| S | Y | N | C | O | P | A | T | I | O | N | M | R |
| H | S | S | A | G | L | T | N | E | M | V | P | E |
| A | F | D | L | H | D | J | F | I | R | P | O | P |
| R | L | K | F | C | E | R | F | H | I | G | K | E |
| P | O | D | I | M | I | N | U | E | N | D | O | A |
| G | I | N | N | R | E | G | N | A | R | R | A | T |
| D | H | H | E | N | N | A | T | U | R | A | L | B |

# Lesson 18

*Fingerboard Power!* A new house is also going in on the D string between 1ˢᵗ and 2ⁿᵈ finger. "E" up to "F♯" is a whole step. Another house can fit between them! This is "F♮" or "F." "F♮" is a half step above "E." 2ⁿᵈ finger plays both "F♮" and "F♯."

1. Write the letters in each house on the D string.

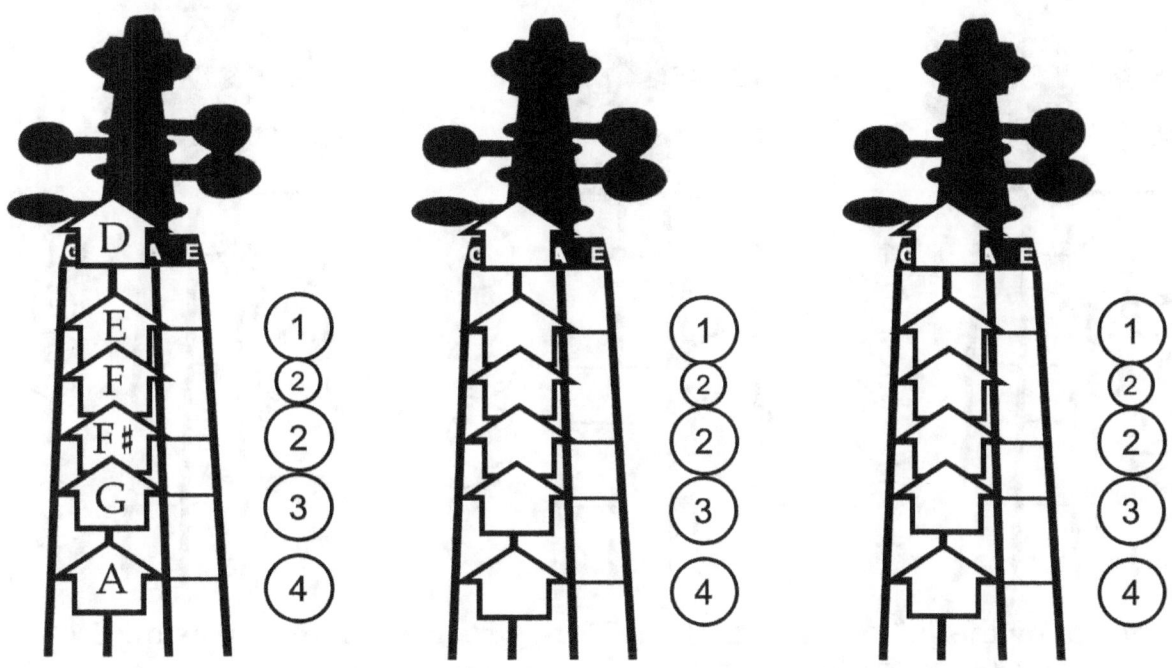

If there is a sharp by the "F" on the staff, then 2ⁿᵈ finger plays a half step below 3ʳᵈ finger "G." If there is not a sharp, then 2ⁿᵈ finger plays a half step above 1ˢᵗ finger "E." This is another "low 2."

"F" is a chromatic half step lower than "F♯," so both "F♮" and "F♯" are in space 1.

2. Draw a treble clef. Trace the "F♮" on the staff and draw 2 more. Remember to draw the natural on the left side of the note head. Draw another treble clef, and trace the "F♯" on the staff and draw 2 more.

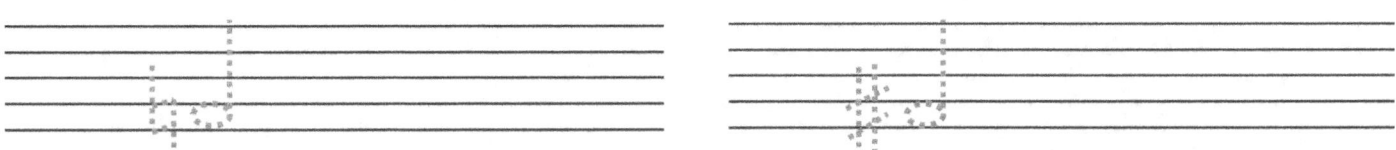

A new house is also going in on the G string between 1ˢᵗ and 2ⁿᵈ finger. "A" up to "B" is a whole step. Another house can fit between them! This is "B♭." "B♭" is a half step below "B♮." 2ⁿᵈ finger plays both "B♭" and "B♮."

3. Write the letters in each house on the G string.

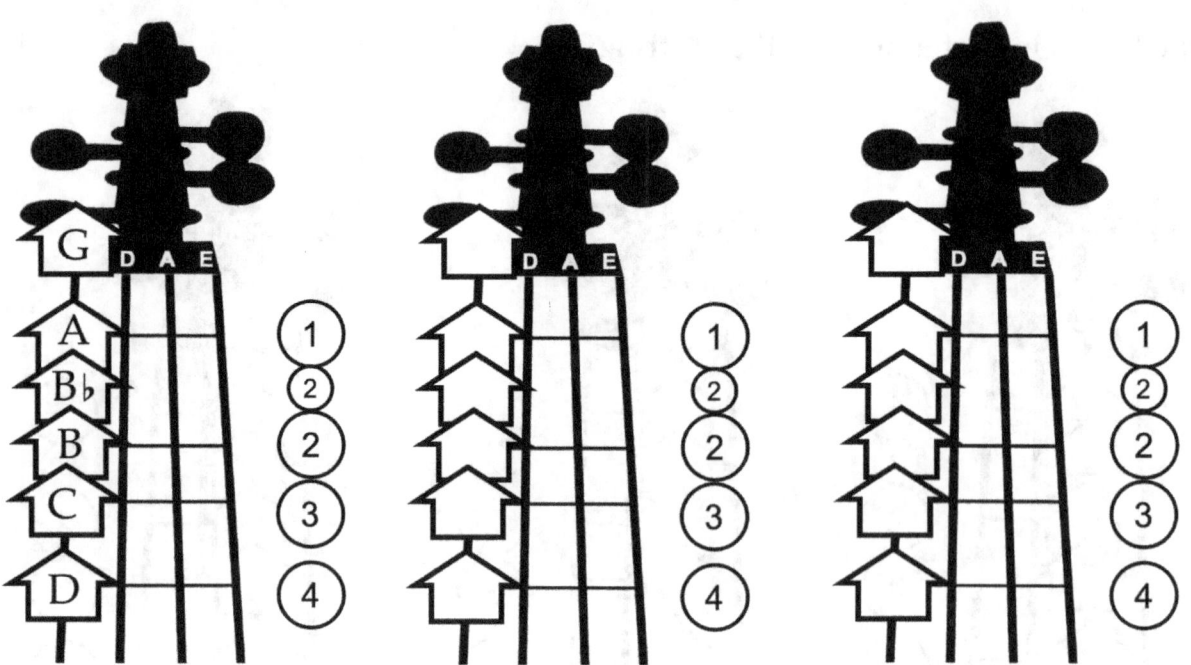

If there is no flat by the "B" on the staff, then 2ⁿᵈ finger plays a half step below 3ʳᵈ finger "G." If there is a flat by "B," then 2ⁿᵈ finger plays a half step above 1ˢᵗ finger "A."

"B♭" is a chromatic half step lower than "B♮," so both "B" and "B♭" sit under ledger line 1, below the staff.

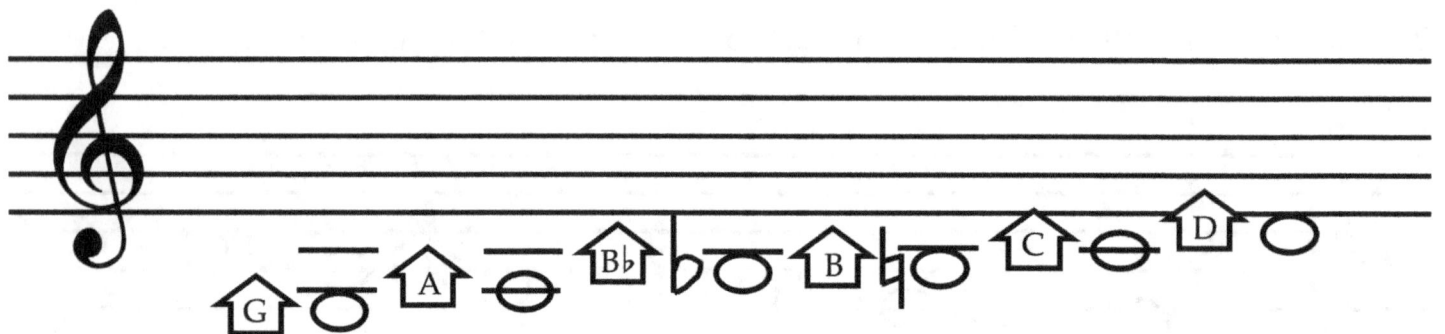

4. Draw a treble clef. Trace the "B♭" on the staff and draw 2 more. Remember to draw the natural on the left side of the note. Draw another treble clef, and trace the "B♮" on the staff and draw 2 more.

The Magic of Music Theory Book 2 - © 2025 Horsehair Music. Photocopying prohibited.

# Lesson 19

When the chromatic signs are used to change a note, they are called **accidentals**. (Though they aren't there by accident!)

## Chromatic Sign Rules:

1. An accidental applies to that pitch for the rest of the measure, unless a natural cancels it.
2. A natural cancels a sharp or flat. Naturals show that the note is changing.
3. A bar line cancels an accidental. The accidental must be rewritten in the next measure.

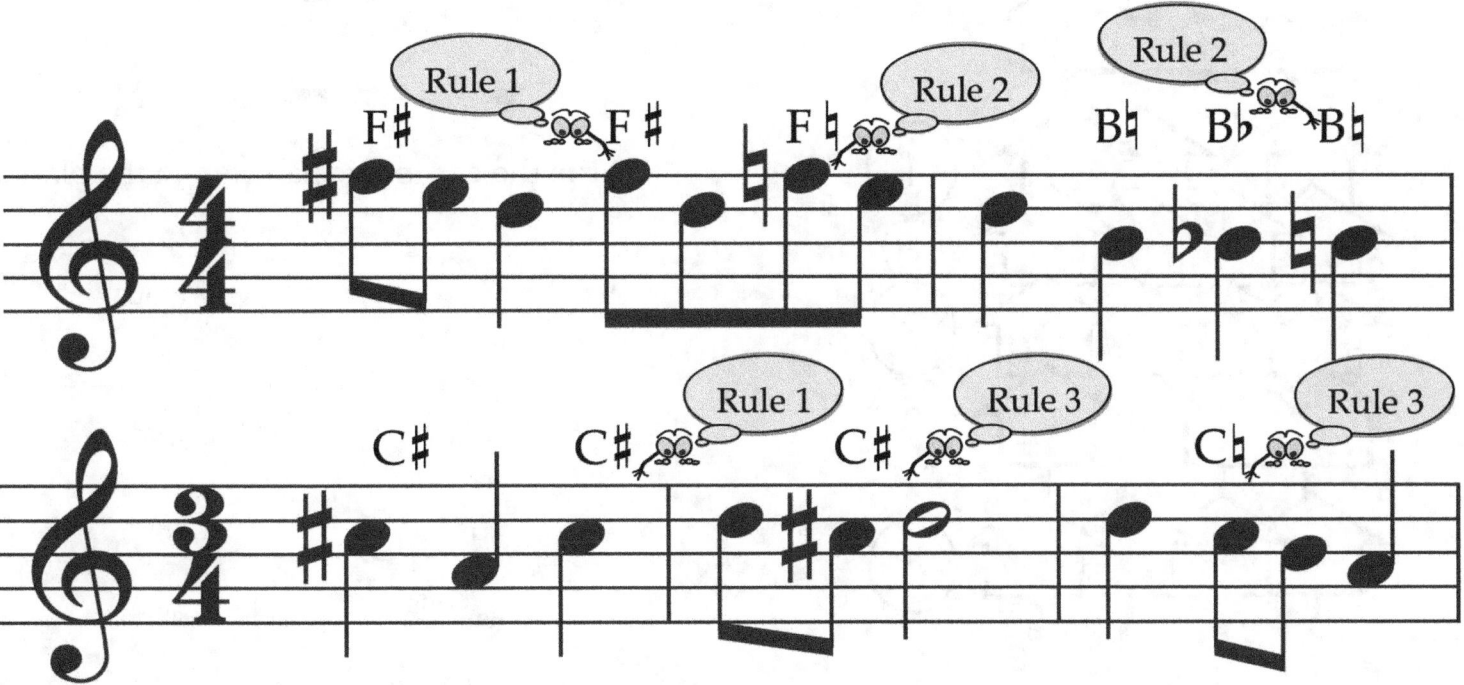

1. Write the letter name with its chromatic sign on the line for each circled note.

Ludwig van Beethoven, Minuet, WoO 10

Johann Sebastian Bach, Concerto in D Minor for 2 Violins, BWV 1043, I. Vivace

2. Write the letters in each house on the fingerboard.

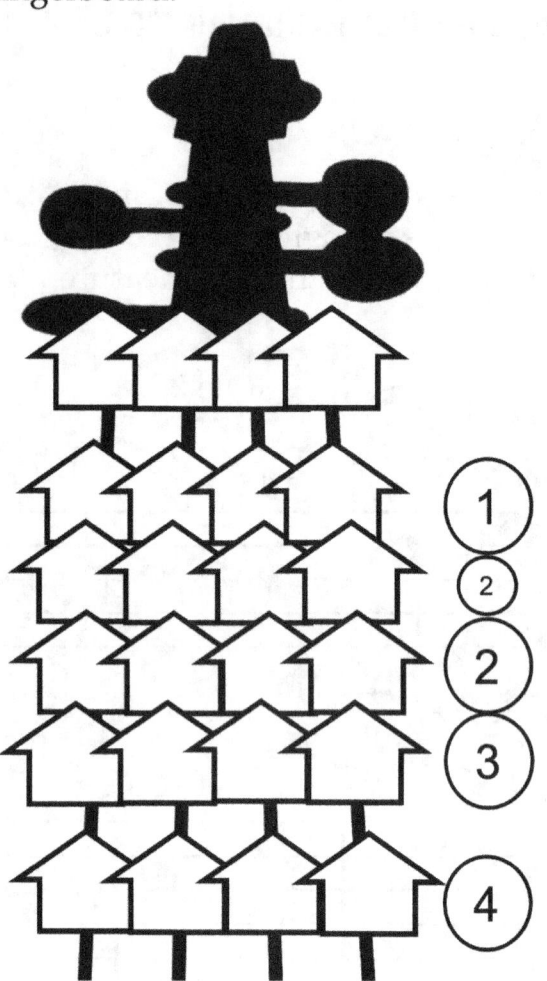

3. Draw a line from the note or rest to the number of beats it receives.

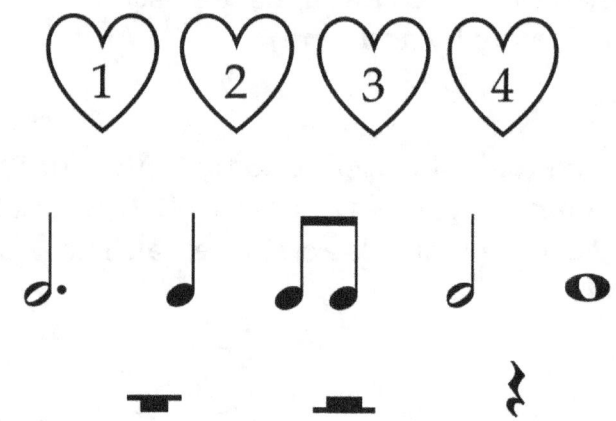

4. Write the chromatic half step in the blank.

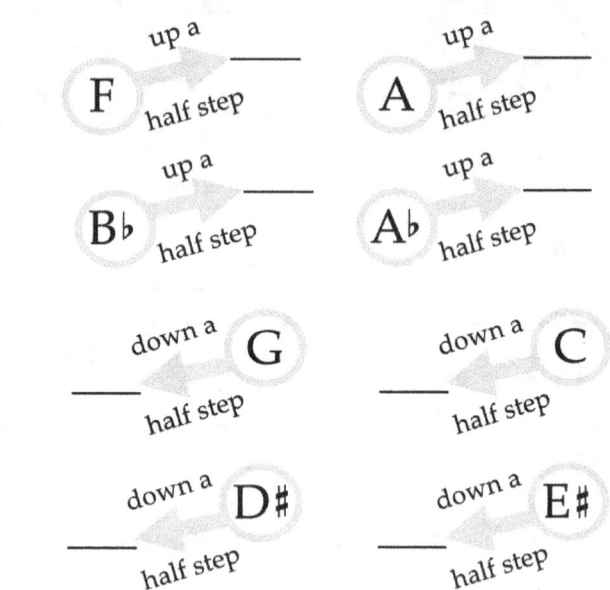

5. Say and clap each picture. Decide if the pattern you clap is ♩ ♫ or ♫ ♩. Then, draw the pattern on the line.

 **Panda Bear**      **Rocking Chair**      **Hot Chocolate**

_____     _____     _____

**Maple Leaf**      **Blank Paper**      **Sandcastle**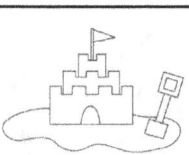

_____     _____     _____

# What do you hear? #6

Music creates a mood or feeling. Two of the tools that composers use to create a mood are called **major** and **minor**. Music in a major key sounds happy. Music in a minor key sounds spooky, sad, or sometimes angry.

Listen to your teacher play the first 5 notes of a major scale. Then, listen to your teacher play the first 5 notes of a minor scale. Do you hear the difference? Just changing one note makes it sound very different!

Major                    Minor

You will hear 5 notes stepping up. If the notes you hear are major, circle major and the happy face emoji. If the 5 notes you hear are minor, circle minor and the sad face emoji.

The teacher may choose from these examples for questions 1 - 5.

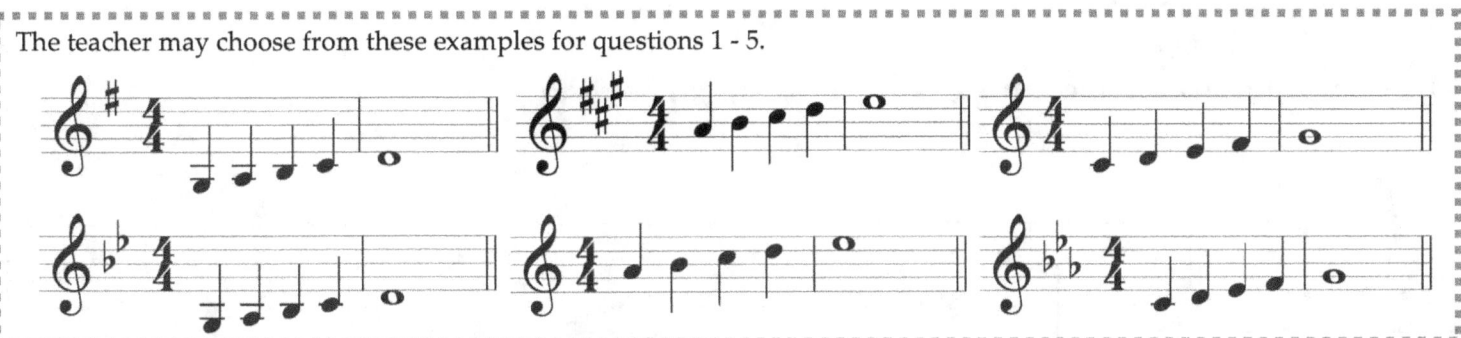

# Lesson 20

1. Draw a line from the name to the correct part of the bow.

tip   horsehair   stick   wrapping   grip   ferrule   frog   eye   screw

2. Fill in the blanks.

◻ is the symbol for _____ bow.      ⋁ is the symbol for _____ bow.

How a note starts and ends is called **articulation.** Articulations are made with the bow. Two types of articulations are legato and staccato. **Legato** means smooth and connected with no space between the notes. **Staccato** means short or detached. Staccato is marked in music with dots above or below the note head.

3. Draw a staccato dot on each quarter note.

Ignatius Sancho, Just So in the North

Legato means smooth and connected. String players play legato as smooth separate bows or by slurring. A **slur** is 2 or more notes on 1 bow stroke. A **slur** is a curved line connecting the note heads. Slurs can go above or below the staff. If the stems are different directions, the slur is drawn drawn above the staff.

4. Draw 1 slur in each measure to slur all the eighth notes together.

Charles de Bériot, Air Varie No. 14

The Magic of Music Theory Book 2 - © 2025 Horsehair Music. Photocopying prohibited.

A **hooked bow** looks like a slur, but there are also staccato dots by the note head. The bow stops between the notes but keeps going the same direction for the second note. It is a down (stop) down, or an up (stop) up.

Ludwig van Beethoven, Minuet, WoO 10

5. Copy the the slurs and hooked bows from the example above into the music below.

Ludwig van Beethoven, Minuet, WoO 10

6. Draw in the hooked bows (staccato dots and slurs) that are shown by the bow markings.

Carl Maria von Weber, arr. Willy Burmester, Waltz

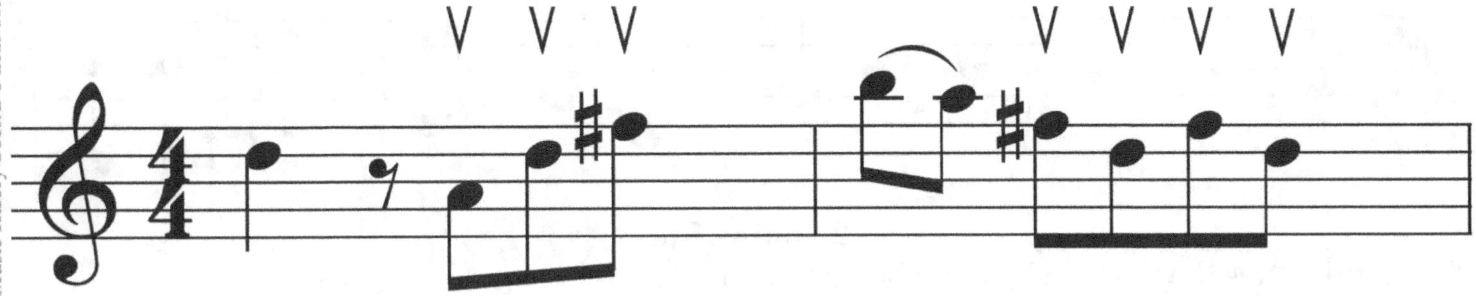

Josephine Trott, At Dancing School

Johannes Brahms, Sonata No. 1 in G Major, I. Vivace ma non troppo

# Lesson 21

1. Draw the stems and beams to make eighth notes. Then, mark the articulations. (Review eighth note stem and beam rules on p 29.)

Beaming eighth notes together makes it easier for our eyes to track and read music. Beams group the notes into beats. Look at the two examples below. The pitches and rhythm are identical. The difference is that the first example uses flags the second example uses beams.

### Beaming Rules

☐ Eighth notes that share a beat are beamed together.
☐ Beam more than one beat of eighth notes together but never beam across a bar line.
☐ Never beam across the the middle of a measure.

2. Add stems and beams, beaming 4 eighth notes together. Then, add staccato dots to each note.

Wolfgang Amadeus Mozart, Sonata in D Major for Piano and Violin, K. 306, I. Allegro con spirito

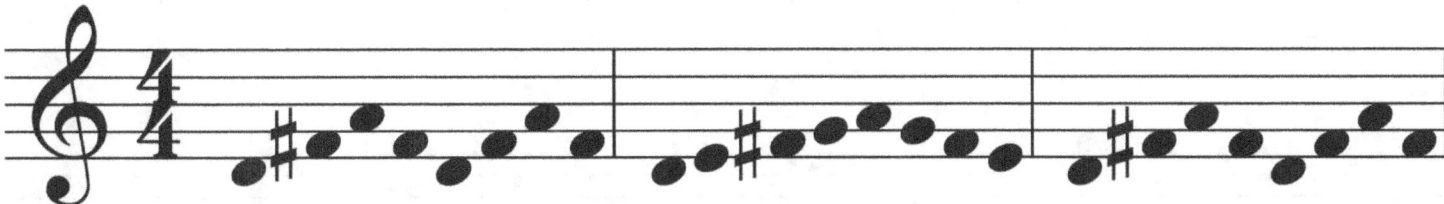

3. Add stems and beams, beaming 4 eighth notes together. Then, draw 1 slur, slurring all the notes in each measure together.

Ludwig van Beethoven, Sonata in A Major for Piano and Cello, I. Allegro ma non tanto

4. Add stems and beams, beaming 4 eighth notes together. Then, draw two-note slurs for all the eighth notes.

Wolfgang Amadeus Mozart, Duos for Violin and Viola, No. 1, I. Allegro

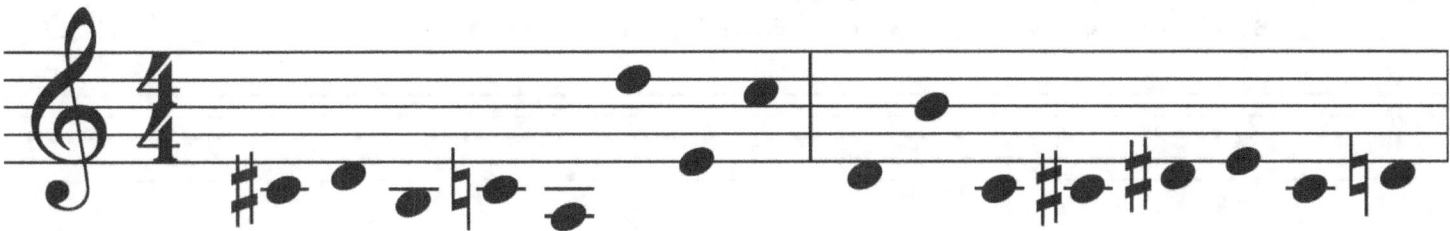

5. The hearts are gone! Write only the counts on the lines. (If you need to write how many beats each note gets, what is usually in the hearts, pencil it in above the note.)

Franz Schubert, Arpeggione Sonata, I. Allegro moderato

Counts: _ _ _ _ _ _ _ _ _ _ _ _ _ _

Max Bruch, Four Pieces for Cello and Piano, I. Aria

Counts: _ _ _ _ _ _ _ _ _ _ _ _ _ _

### *Discover the Composers*

10. Fill in the letters of the notes to learn about the life of a great composer while you listen to Mozart's Divertimento in D major, I. Allegro, K. 136. Listen to see if you hear the minor section.

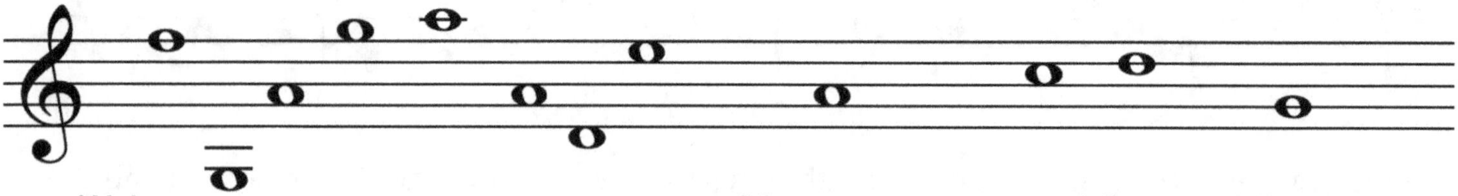

Wol___ ___ ___n___ ___m___ ___ ___us Moz___rt was a ___hil___ prodi___y.

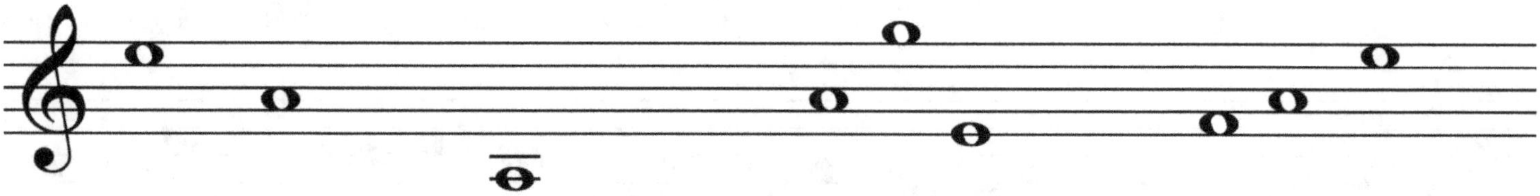

H___ beg___n taking pi___no lessons at ___ ___ ___ 3 from his ___ ___th___r.

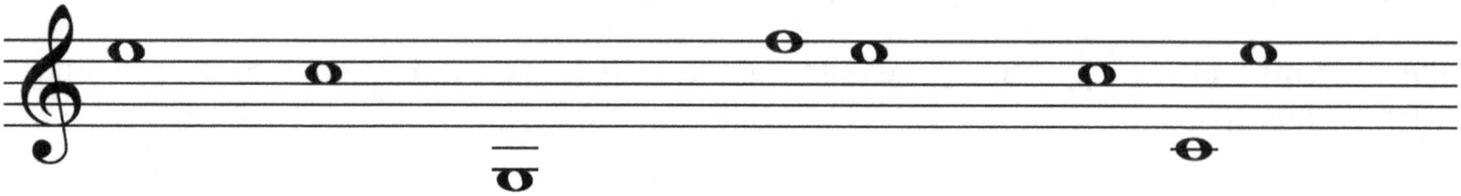

H___ started ___omposin___ when he was ___iv___. He gave ___on___ ___rts to kings

and prin___ ___s all over Europe. Moz___rt compos___ ___ almost 1000 pieces in his

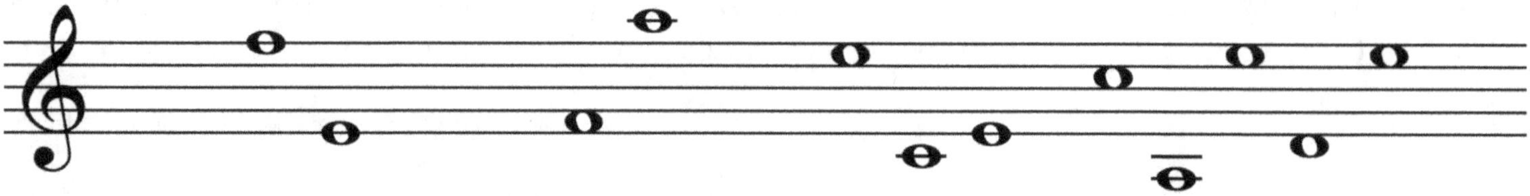

very short li___ ___. One of his ___ ___ mous pi___ ___ ___s is ___ ___ll___ ___ "___ine

Kl___in___ N___ ___ht Musik." It m___ ___ns ___ Little Ni___ht Music. He ___ i___ ___

___ ___ ___or___ ___inishin___ his l___st work ___ ___ll___d "R___qui___m."

The Magic of Music Theory Book 2 - © 2025 Horsehair Music. Photocopying prohibited.

# Lesson 22

*Fingerboard Power!* More new houses are going in on the fingerboard. There is room for a house on all the strings between 3rd finger and 4th finger. But 3rd and 4th fingers have decided to share these houses. Sometimes 3rd finger (high 3) will live here, sometimes 4th finger (low 4) will use it. This means that one house can have 2 different letter names! There are many reasons and rules that guide composers to choose whether a note is called by a flat name or a sharp name. You must know both names for the fingerboard house.

1. Write in both letter names for each gray house on the blank fingerboard.

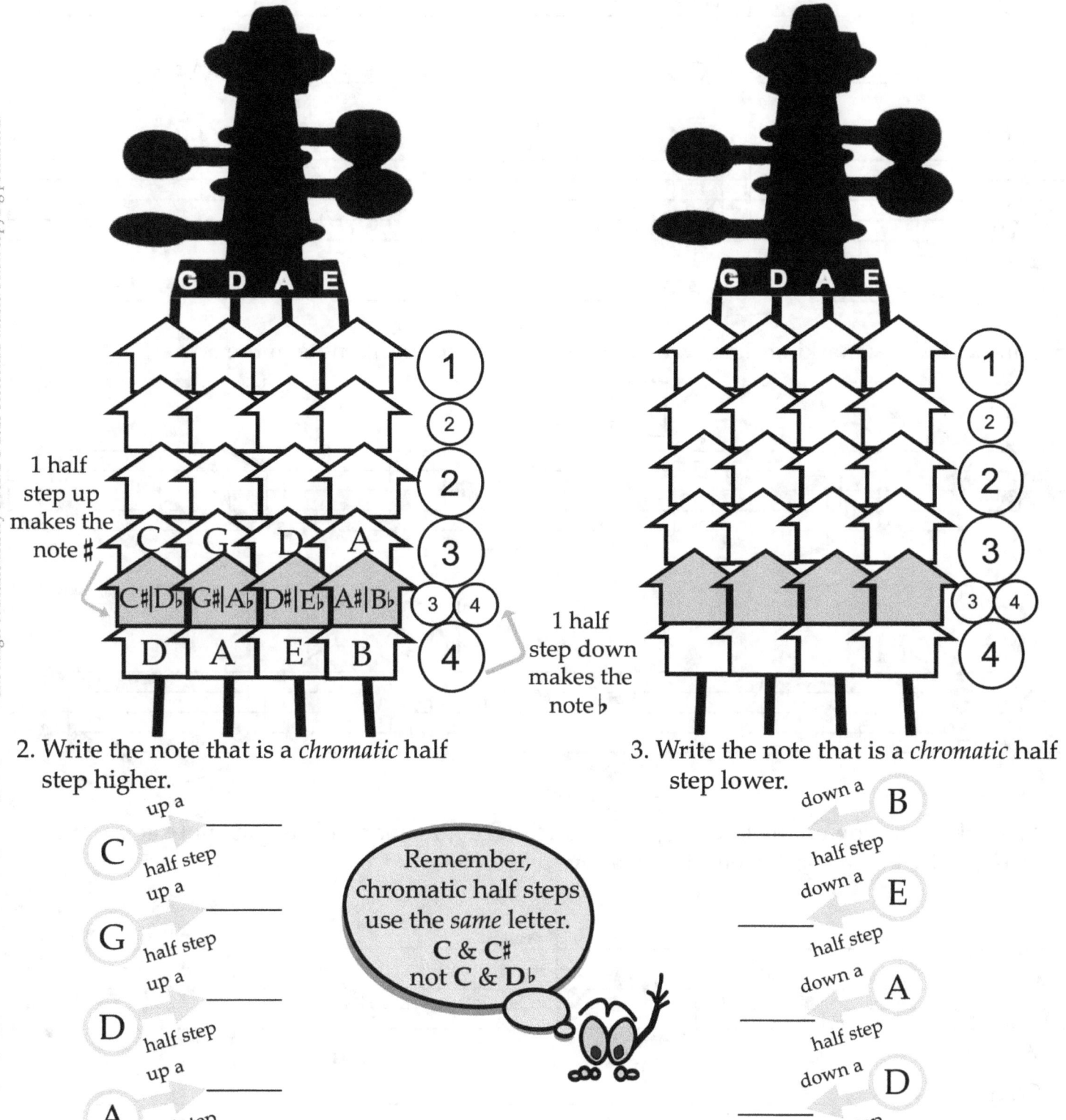

1 half step up makes the note #

1 half step down makes the note ♭

2. Write the note that is a *chromatic* half step higher.

C up a _____ half step

G up a _____ half step

D up a _____ half step

A up a _____ half step

Remember, chromatic half steps use the *same* letter. **C & C#** not **C & D♭**

3. Write the note that is a *chromatic* half step lower.

down a B _____ half step

down a E _____ half step

down a A _____ half step

down a D _____ half step

We call notes that have *different* letter names but live in the *same house* and *sound the same* - **enharmonic notes**. It's like they have secret spy names. Sometimes they go by their flat name, and sometimes they use their sharp name!

D#

Eb

4. Write the enharmonic name on the line and draw the note on the staff as a half note.

C# = _____    G# = _____    D# = _____    A# = _____

Db = _____    Ab = _____    Eb = _____    Bb = _____

5. Follow the bow markings and write the bow direction for that note in the box.

Irma Seydel, Minuet

Ernest Chausson, Piece, Op. 39

6. Write the counting on the lines. If you need to write how many beats each note gets (what is normally in the hearts), pencil it in above each note.

Maurice Ravel, Sonata for Violin and Cello, I. Allegro

Counts: _ _ _ _   _ _ _ _   _ _ _ _

The Magic of Music Theory Book 2 - © 2025 Horsehair Music. Photocopying prohibited.

62

# Lesson 23

A **scale** is made up of 8 notes. The first note and the last note of the scale are the same letter. It follows a pattern of whole steps (Whole or W) and half steps (Half or H). **ALWAYS step up to the next letter in the music alphabet when building a scale.**

The major scale pattern is :

Begin   Whole   Whole   Half   Whole   Whole   Whole   Half
        ( W )   ( W )   ( H )   ( W )   ( W )   ( W )   ( H )

A silly sentence can help you remember this pattern:
- **We Worked Hard, When We Worked Hard.**
- **Willy Wonka Had Wee Willi Winky Honk.**
- **Wally Won't Help When Whitney Won't Help**

1. Write the major scale pattern below. (Use "W's" and "H's")

     Begin  \_\_\_\_\_  \_\_\_\_\_  \_\_\_\_\_  \_\_\_\_\_  \_\_\_\_\_  \_\_\_\_\_  \_\_\_\_\_

2. Make your own silly sentence using words that start with "W" and "H" to help you remember the major scale pattern.

_____

3. Look at the fingerboard and fill in the gray box with the letters for the C Major Scale.

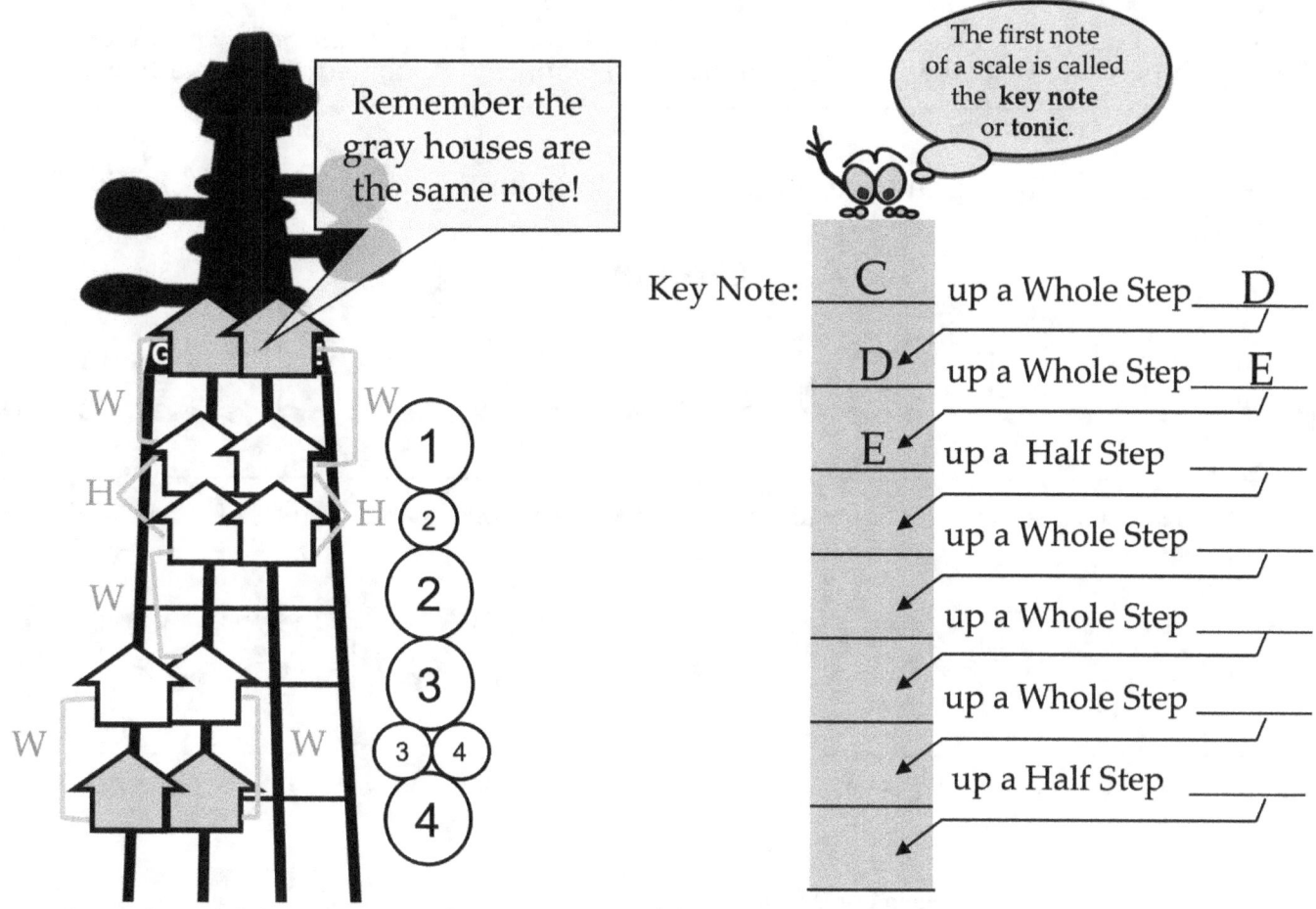

Remember the gray houses are the same note!

The first note of a scale is called the **key note** or **tonic**.

Key Note: \_\_\_C\_\_\_ up a Whole Step\_\_\_D\_\_\_

D up a Whole Step\_\_\_E\_\_\_

E up a Half Step \_\_\_\_\_

up a Whole Step \_\_\_\_\_

up a Whole Step \_\_\_\_\_

up a Whole Step \_\_\_\_\_

up a Half Step \_\_\_\_\_

5. Write the letters for the C major scale in the blanks.

_ C _ ⇑W ____ ⇑W ____ ⇑H ____ ⇑W ____ ⇑W ____ ⇑W ____ ⇑H _ C _

6. Look at the pitches in #5 and draw the C major scale on the staff using whole notes.

7. Did you use any sharps or flats?    YES    NO

8. The C scale has _____, _____, _____.
  (number)   (sharps or flats)   (name the sharps or flats)

9. Play the C scale on your violin. Say the letters *out loud* while you play.

**? ? Did you know???**
The first note in the scale is called the **key note** or **tonic.** Each note in the scale has a different name depending on its position in the scale.

| 1st note | 2nd note | 3rd note | 4th note | 5th note | 6th note | 7th note |
|---|---|---|---|---|---|---|
| Tonic | Supertonic | Mediant | Subdominant | Dominant | Submediant | Leading tone |

10. Choose notes from the C scale and compose a melody for the poem "Clouds." Begin and end on C.

**Clouds**

White sheep, white sheep,   On a blue hill,   When the wind stops,   You all stand still.

When the wind blows, You  walk a-way slow.   White sheep, white sheep, Where do you go?

Words: Anonymous, Music:_____
                                    (Your Name)

The Magic of Music Theory Book 2 - © 2025 Horsehair Music. Photocopying prohibited.

# Lesson 24

1. Write the major scale pattern below. (Use "W's" and "H's")

Begin _____  _____  _____  _____  _____  _____  _____

2. Look at the fingerboard and fill in the blanks for the G Major Scale.

_G_ ⇑W _____ ⇑W _____ ⇑H _____ ⇑W _____ ⇑W _____ ⇑W _____ ⇑H _G_

3. Did you use any sharps or flats?    YES    NO

4. The G scale has _____, _____,
                    (number)    (sharps or flats)

which is _____.
            (name the sharps or flats)

5. What is the key note for the G major scale? _____

6. Play the G scale on your violin. Say the letters *out loud* while you play.

7. Draw a treble clef. Then, draw the scale on the staff using whole notes. (Remember, chromatic signs are drawn on the left side of the note head.)

8. Look at the fingerboard and fill in the blanks for the D Major Scale.

_D_ ⇑W _____ ⇑W _____ ⇑H _____ ⇑W _____ ⇑W _____ ⇑W _____ ⇑H _D_

9. Did you use any sharps or flats?    YES    NO

10. The D scale has _____, _____,
                    (number)    (sharps or flats)

which is _____.
            (name the sharps or flats)

11. What is the key note for the D major scale? _____

12. Play the D scale on your violin. Say the letters *out loud* while you play.

13. On page 66, draw a treble clef. Then, draw the D scale on the staff using whole notes. (Chromatic signs go on the left side of the note head.)

65

14. Look at the fingerboard and fill in the blanks for the A Major Scale.

_A_ ⇑W _____ ⇑W _____ ⇑H _____ ⇑W _____ ⇑W _____ ⇑W _____ ⇑H _A_

15. Did you use any sharps or flats?    YES    NO

16. The A scale has _____, _____,
                 (number)    (sharps or flats)

    which is _____.
                 (name the sharps or flats)

17. What is the key note for the A major scale? _____

18. Play the A scale on your violin. Say the letters *out loud* while you play.

19. Draw a treble clef. Draw the A scale on the staff using whole notes. (Chromatic signs go on the left side of the note head.)

20. Draw a line from the key note to its matching house.

The Magic of Music Theory Book 2 – © 2023 Horsehair Music. Photocopying prohibited.

# Lesson 25

Fill in the number of sharps for each key:

1. C Scale has _____ sharps.     2. G Scale has _____ sharp.

3. D Scale has _____ sharps.     4. A Scale has _____ sharps.

In major scales the half steps are always between the 3rd and 4th notes and the 7th and 8th notes of the scale. To mark a half step between notes, draw a little tent between the note heads.

## Scaly

Adagio

Al - li - ga - tors, liz - ards,     arm - a - dil - los,  mam - bas,

croc - o - di - les, tur - tles,     but - ter - flies, i - guan - as,

all of these have sca - les,     but what do 'ya know,

fin - ger - boards have sca - les     played a - da - gi - o

C  D  E  F  G  A  B  C    Beats:

Counts: __ __ __ __

G  A  B  C  D  E  F#  G    Beats:

Counts: __ __ __ __

D  E  F#  G  A  B  C#  D    Beats:

Counts: __ __ __

A  B  C#  D  E  F#  G#  A    Beats:

Counts: __ __ __ __

5. Write the notes of each scale as quarter notes.

6. Write the number of beats for each rest in the hearts, and the counts on the lines.

7. Draw a tent between the half steps (notes 3 & 4 and 7 & 8) on *each* scale.

NOT fingers 3 and 4 but notes 3 and 4 of the scale.

8. Adagio means _____.

9. Play Scaly on your violin.

68

# SPOT IT

**BEFORE YOU START:**
Cut out the circles on page 67, 69, and 71.

## GAME 1: TWINS

SET UP:
Place all the cards face down in a pile in the middle.

HOW TO PLAY:
1. Flip two cards over so that all players can see both cards.
2. Players try to spot the matching symbol on both cards.
3. When you find the matching symbol, call out the name of that symbol.
4. The person who calls it out first, takes those two cards.
5. Flip two more cards over and repeat the steps until no cards are left.

HOW TO WIN:
The person with the most cards wins.

## GAME 2: THE TOWER

SET UP:
1. Place one card face down in front of each player.
2. Place the remaining cards in a stack face up in the middle.

HOW TO PLAY:
1. On the count of three, all players flip over their cards.
2. Players try to spot the matching symbol from the card in front of them with the card on top of the stack in the middle.
3. The player who finds the matching symbol should call out the name of that symbol.
4. The person who calls it out first, takes the card in the middle.
5. Look for the matching symbol on the next card in the stack.

HOW TO WIN:
The person with the most cards wins.

# What do you hear? #7

Listen to a recording of Mozart's "Eine Kliene Nachtmusik" [Eye-neh Kline-neh Knock-t Muze-eek], I. Allegro (K. 525). Listen to the melody played by the 1st violins. Each time you hear staccato notes, draw a tick under staccato. Each time you hear legato notes, draw a tick under legato.

| Staccato | Legato |
|---|---|
|  |  |

What instruments played this piece? _____

What is this group of instruments called? _____

Do you think this piece sounds happy or sad?_____ Was

this piece fast or slow? _____ Mozart marked the tempo

as Allegro. What does Allegro mean? _____. "Eine" is an article

in German that means, "a." "Kleine" translated means "little." "Nacht" means "night, and you can guess what "musik" is. If you were to write the title of this piece in English what would it be?

_____

_____

?? *Did you know???*
A man named Ludwig Ritter von Köchel [Lude-vig rit-ter fon Ker-ckle] organized all of Mozart's compositions and gave each of them a catalogue number. You will see "K." numbers on pieces by Mozart. Since Mozart composed so much, some pieces have the same name "Sonata in C Major." The "K." number helps us know which piece is being referred to.

# Lesson 26

**1. Fill in the letters for the blank houses.**

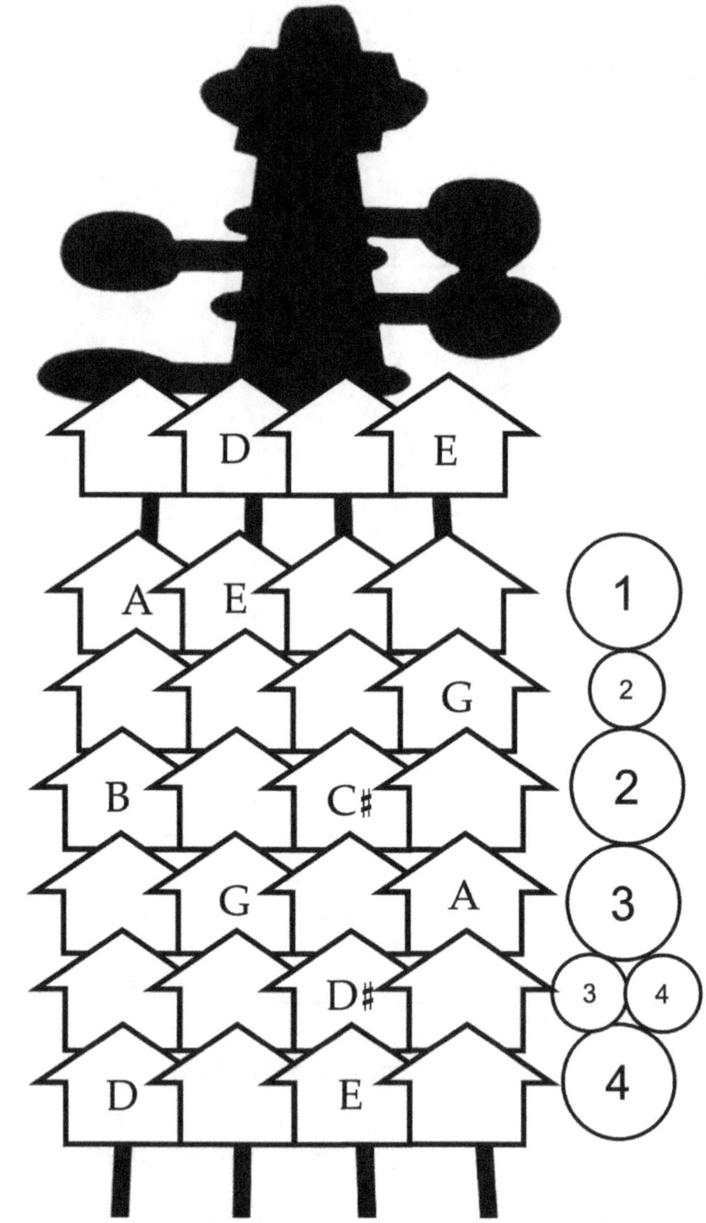

**2. Write the note on the staff that matches the fingerboard house.**

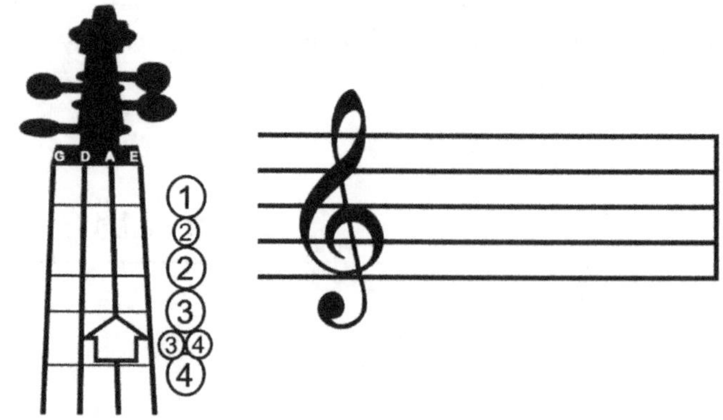

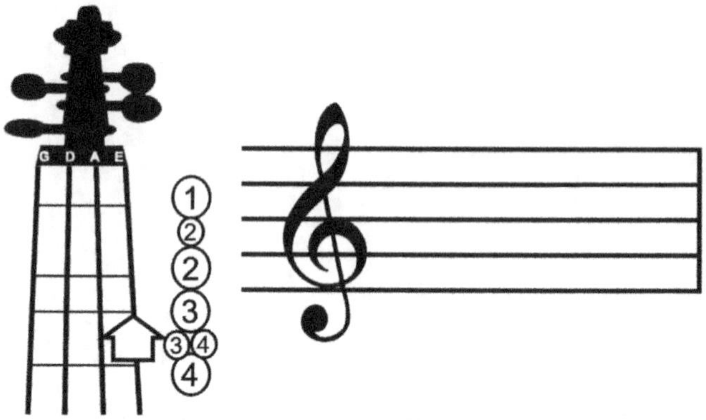

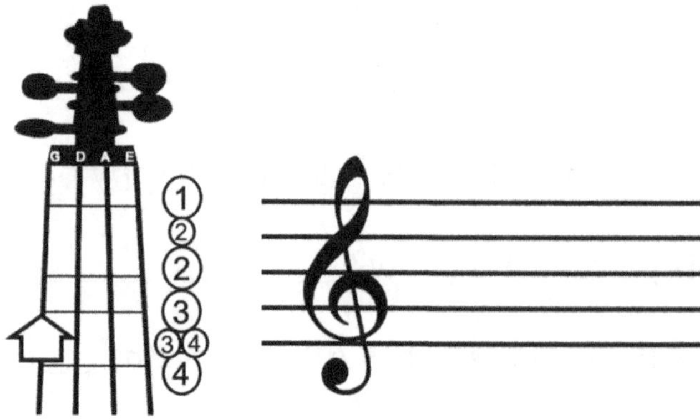

**3. Draw a circle on the fingerboard that matches the note on the staff.**

**Who am I? Write in the letter name.**

4. I am high 3rd finger on the E string? _____

5. I am low 2nd finger on the D string? _____

6. I am low 4th finger on the G string? _____

7. I am high 3rd finger on the D string? _____

8. Write the major scale pattern below. (Use "W's" and "H's")

Begin _____   _____   _____   _____   _____   _____   _____

9. Color the houses on the fingerboard that are used in the G major scale.

10. Color the houses on the fingerboard that are used in a D Major scale.

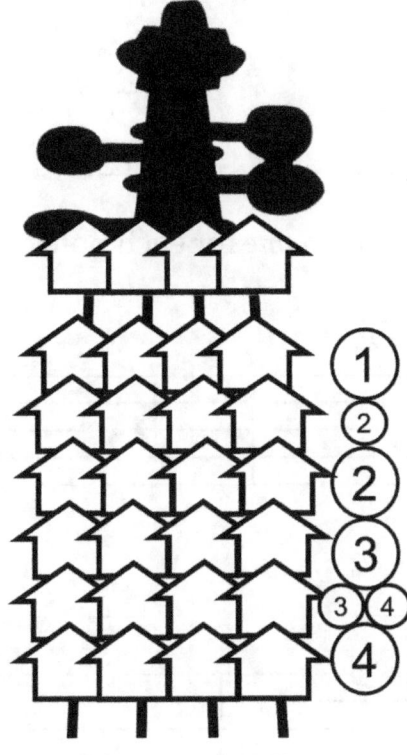

11. Draw a treble clef. Then draw the D Major scale in whole notes on the staff. Don't forget the sharps!

12. Write the letters under each note of the D Major Scale.

77

13. Did any notes have sharps?     yes         no          If yes, what letters? _____
                                          (circle one)

14. On the lines write the *finger number* and the *string* it is found on for each note.

Finger
Number: ___    ___    ___    ___    ___

String: ___    ___    ___    ___    ___

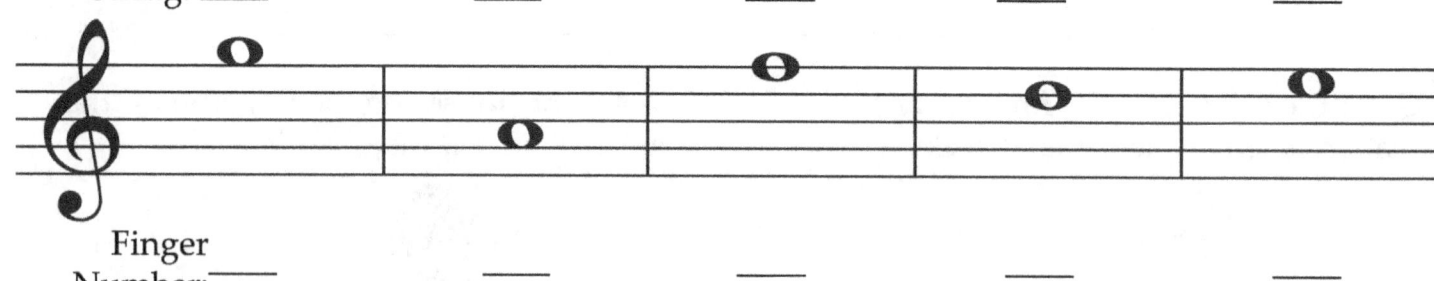

Finger
Number: ___    ___    ___    ___    ___

String: ___    ___    ___    ___    ___

12. Write the *letter name* for each note on the line.

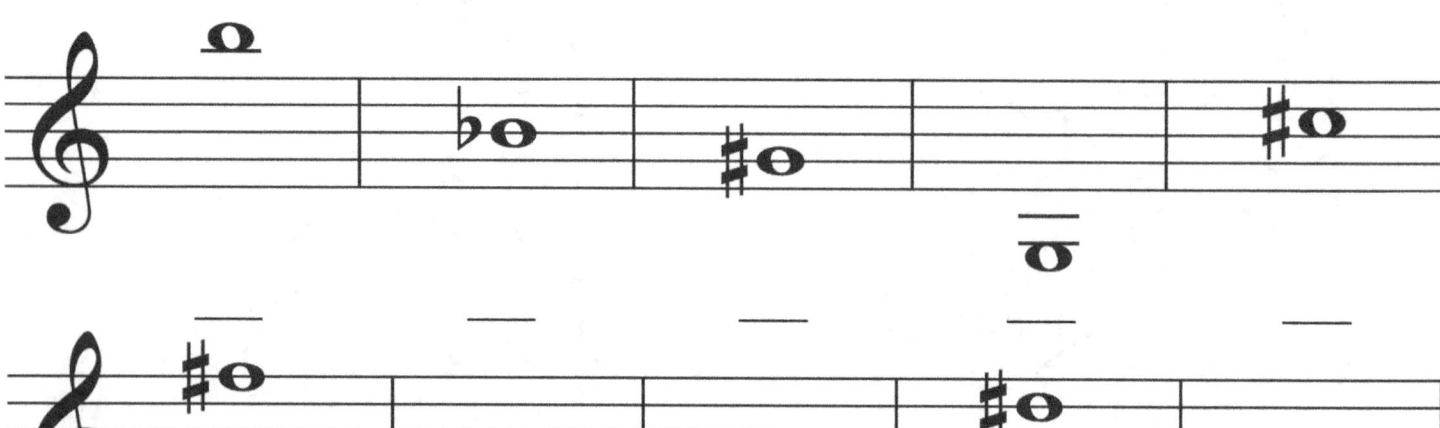

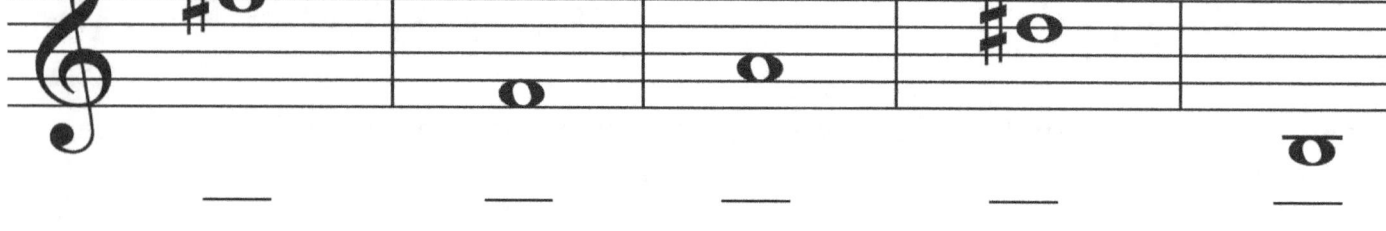

# Lesson 27

When the same note is connected by a curve line it is called a **tie**. A **slur** and a **tie** look the same, but there is one difference – a tie connects notes that are on the *same line or space*. A slur connects notes that are different.

When two notes are tied, we add the beats together and hold the note for the total number of beats. You play a tie like you play a slur with both notes on one bow stroke making it sound like one long note.

1. Write the beats for each note in the hearts and then write the sum in the final heart.

2. Draw a circle around the slurs and a box around the ties.

**Ties** change how we *play* notes, not how we *count* notes.

3. Circle the slurs. Draw a box around the ties. Write the counts on the lines.

Carl Philip Emmanuel Bach, March, BWV 122

Counts: _ _ _ _ _ _ _ _ _ _ _ _ _ _ _ _ _

Jean Gabriel-Marie, La Cinquantaine

Counts: _ _ _ _ _ _ _ _ _ _ _ _ _ _ _ _ _ _

If there is a dot under the slur, this is NOT a tie, even if the two notes are the same! This is a **hooked bow**. The notes are on the same bow stroke, but you stop the bow between notes to rearticulate the second note. This makes it sound like 2 notes.

Christian Petzold, Minuet

4. Circle the slurs. Draw a box around ties. Draw a triangle around hooked bows.

Felix Mendelssohn, String Quartet No. 1, Op. 12, I. Adagio non troppo

The Magic of Music Theory Book 2 - © 2025 Horsehair Music. Photocopying prohibited.

# What do you hear? #8

Listen to a recording of Grieg's "Holberg Suite, Op. 40, No. 3, Gavotte – Musette – Gavotte." Grieg contrasts staccato and legato between the upper strings (violins) and the lower strings (viola, cello, bass.) Listen to this piece two times. The first time listen to the violins. Each time you hear staccato notes, draw a tick under staccato. Each time you hear legato notes, draw a tick under legato.

| Staccato | Legato |
|----------|--------|
|          |        |

Now listen to this piece again and listen for the lower strings. Each time you hear staccato notes, draw a tick under staccato. Each time you hear legato notes, draw a tick under legato.

| Staccato | Legato |
|----------|--------|
|          |        |

Do you think this piece sounds happy

or sad?_____ Is it

major or minor? _____

Was this piece fast or slow? _____

Grieg marked the tempo as Allegretto

What does Allegretto mean?

_____

**?? Did you know???**

In the middle section Grieg marks the tempo as **poco piú mosso**. This is another Italian term composers use to change the tempo.

**poco** = little
**piú** = more
**mosso** = motion

So, this term means play it a little faster with a "little more motion."

81

# Lesson 28

*Fingerboard Power!* There is one more place to put houses on the fingerboard. It is between the nut and the 1st finger tape. Sometimes we call this "low 1." Our first finger moves back to play in this space. These houses also have 2 names (**enharmonic names**). Remember enharmonic notes have different letter but are on the same place on the fingerboard and sound the same!

1. Write both names in the gray houses on the blank fingerboard.

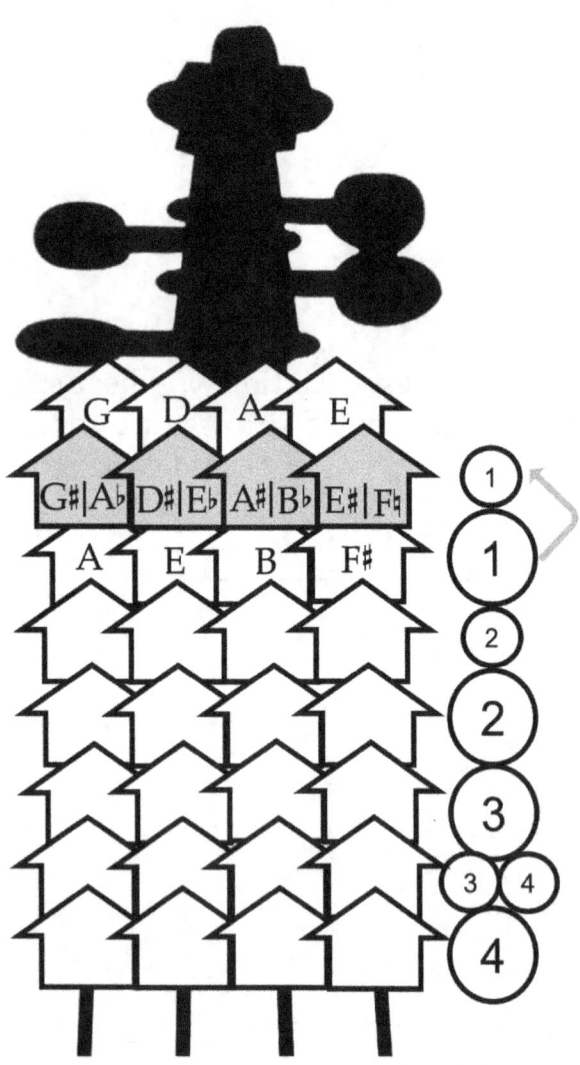
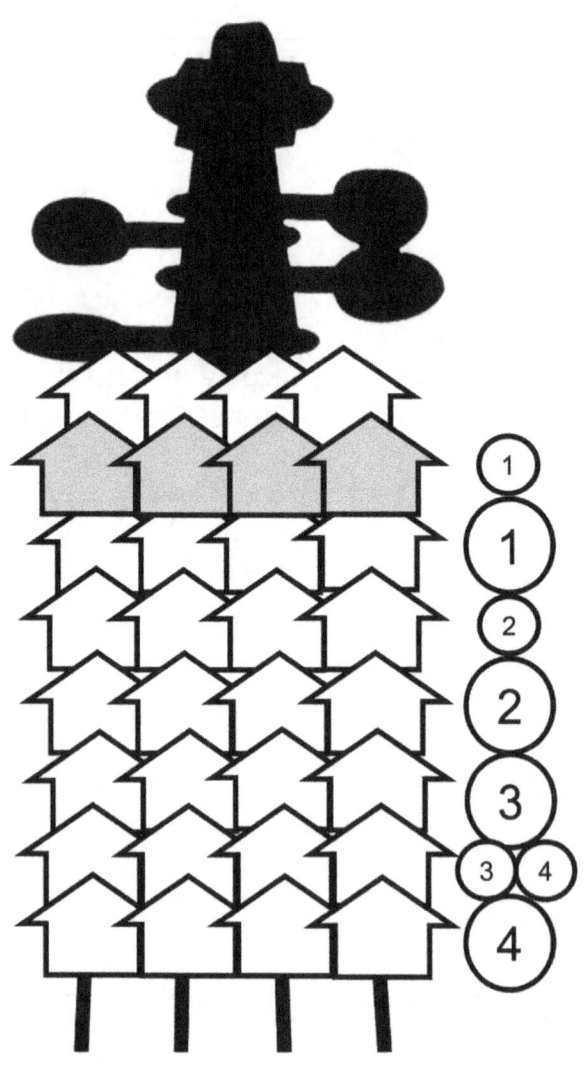

2. Write the note that is a chromatic half step up.

G → up a ___ half step

A → up a ___ half step

D → up a ___ half step

E → up a ___ half step

3. Write the note that is a chromatic half step down

___ ← down a F half step

___ ← down a E half step

___ ← down a B half step

___ ← down a A half step

4. Draw both staff houses that match the fingerboard house as half notes on the staff. Then, write the letter name on the blank.

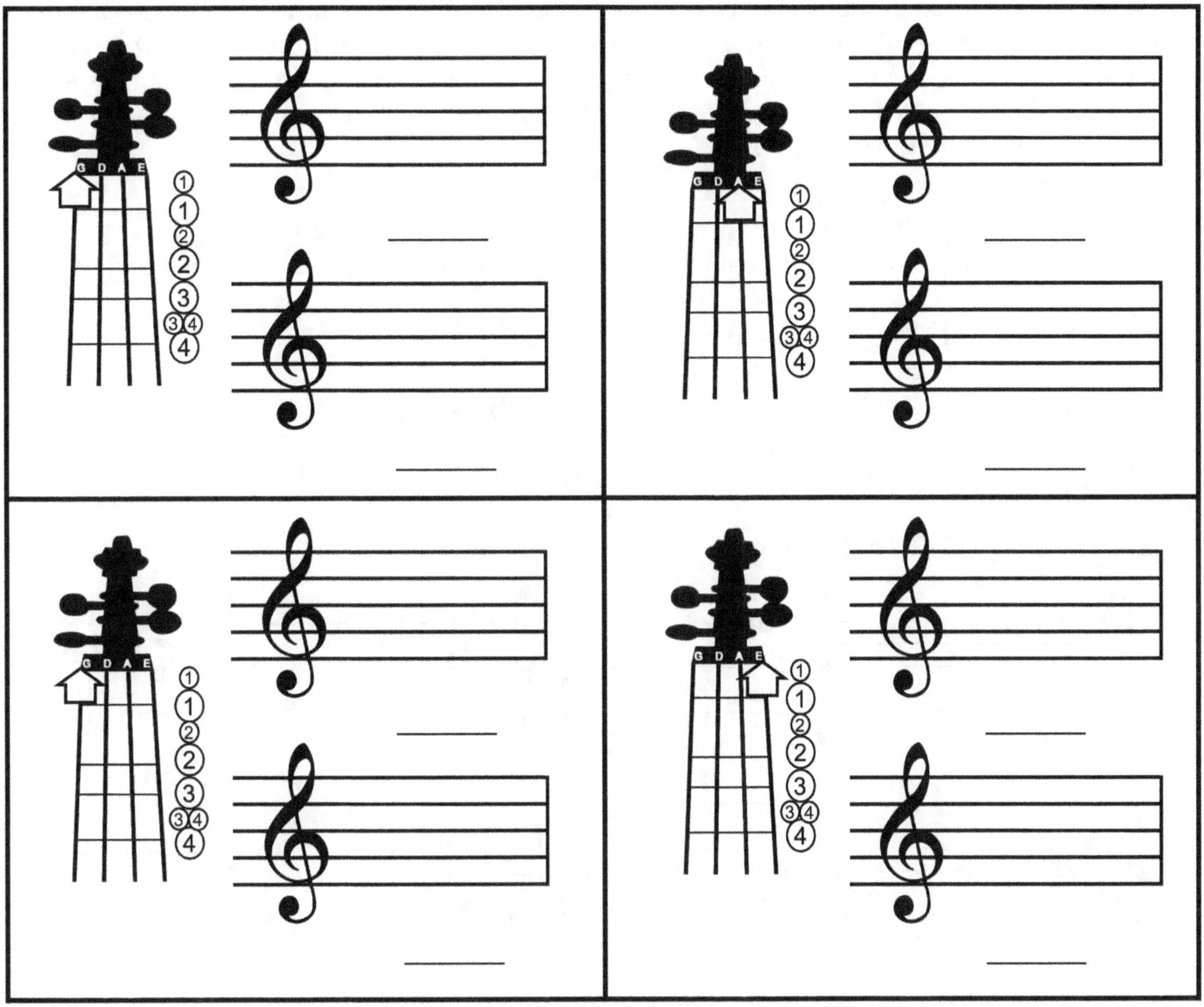

5. Write the counts on the lines. If you need to write how many beats each note gets (what is usually in the hearts), pencil it in above the note.

Antonin Dvořák, Serenade for Strings

Counts: ___ ___ ___ ___ ___ ___ ___ ___ ___ ___

Peter Ilyich Tchaikovsky, Nutcracker, "Arrival of Drosselmeyer"

Counts: ___ ___ ___ ___ ___ ___ ___ ___ ___

# Lesson 29

An **interval** is the distance between two notes. To find an interval, count the number of letters between the two notes. Be sure you include the first letter in your count. A **step** is when you move up or down to the very next letter in the music alphabet. A step covers 2 letters. A step is an interval of a 2nd. A **skip** is when you move up or down by skipping a letter. A skip covers 3 letters. A skip is an interval of a 3rd.

|  |  |
|---|---|
| **Step = 2nd** | **Skip = 3rd** |
| B up to C | B up to D |
| (2 letters B & C = Interval of a 2nd) | (3 letters B, C & D = Interval of a 3rd) |

1. Write the interval (2nd or 3rd) in the blank.

B up to D = _____     G up to A = _____     D up to F = _____     F up to G = _____

E down to D = _____     F down to D = _____     B down to G = _____     A down to F = _____

2. Write the interval (2nd or 3rd) in the blank.

3. Draw a half note that is an interval of a 2nd ABOVE the printed note.

4. Draw an eighth note that is an interval of a 2nd BELOW the printed note.

5. An interval is the _____ between two notes.

84

The Magic of Music Theory Book 2 - © 2025 Horsehair Music. Photocopying prohibited.

6. Draw a quarter note that is an interval of a 3rd ABOVE the printed note.

7. Draw a dotted half note that is an interval of a 3rd BELOW the printed note.

8. Color ALL the houses on the fingerboard that match the letter on the scroll. The first one is done for you.

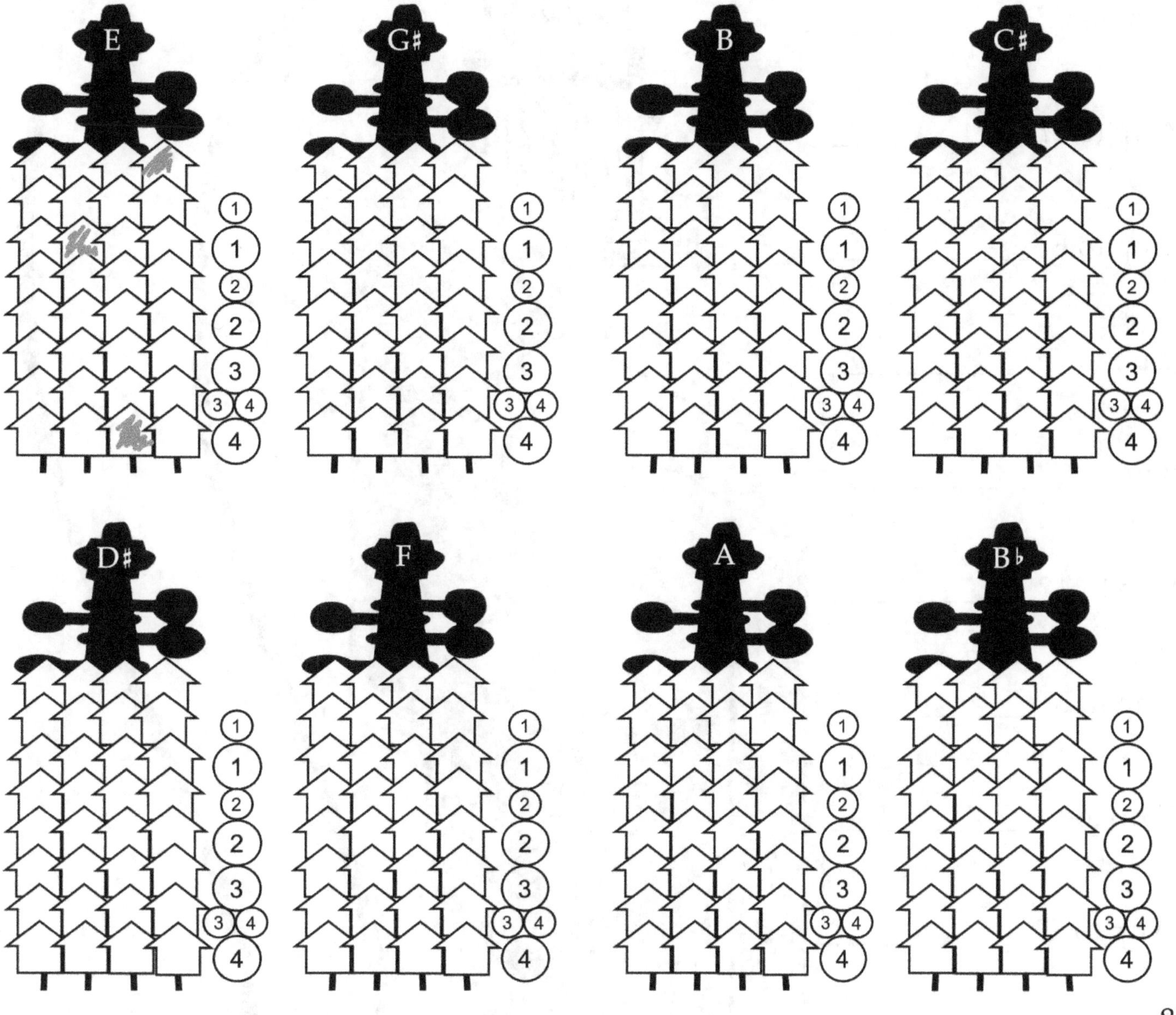

Boxes-'R'-Us has several deliveries. Help the driver find the intervals for the deliveries.

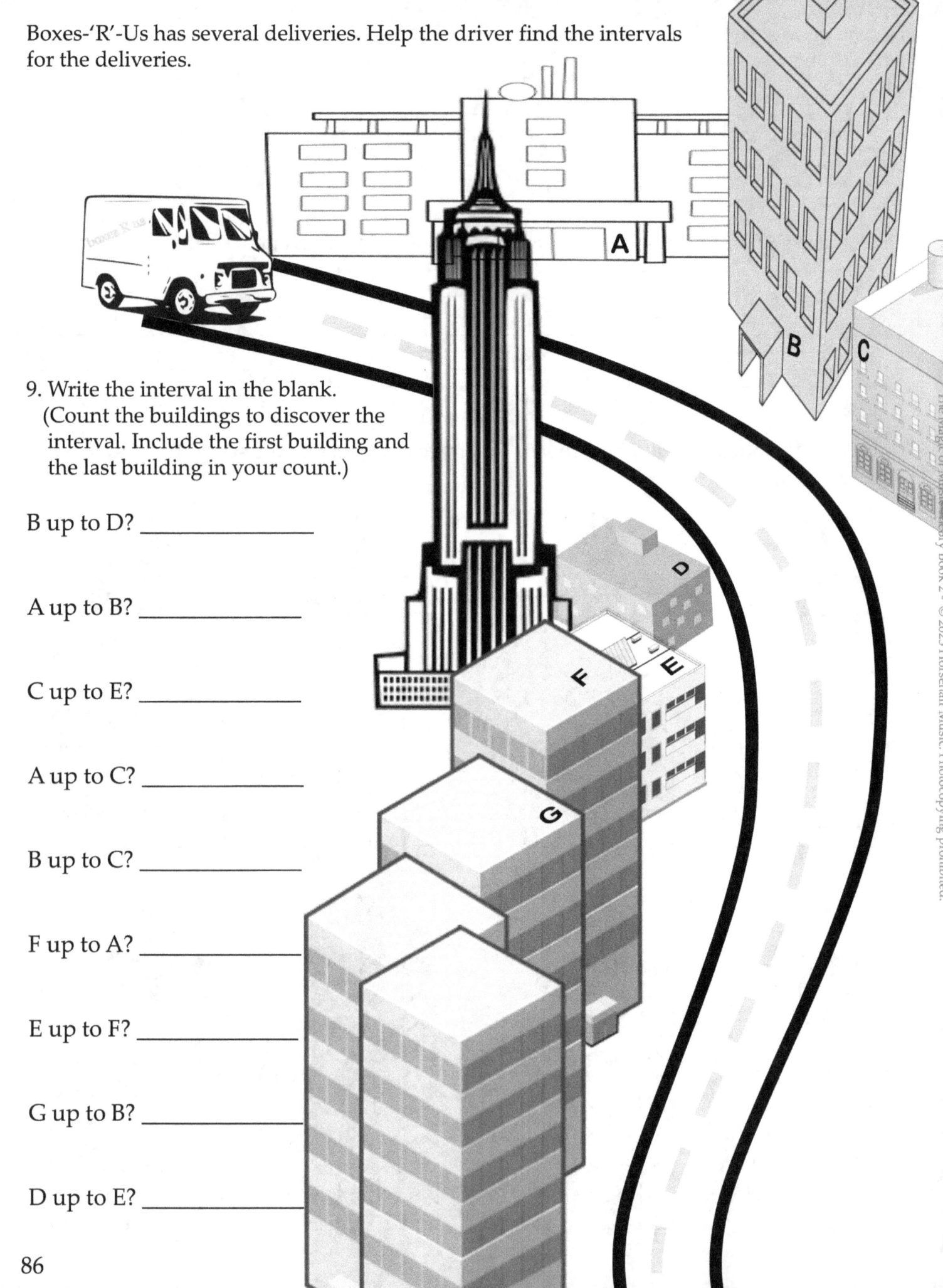

9. Write the interval in the blank.
   (Count the buildings to discover the
   interval. Include the first building and
   the last building in your count.)

B up to D? _____

A up to B? _____

C up to E? _____

A up to C? _____

B up to C? _____

F up to A? _____

E up to F? _____

G up to B? _____

D up to E? _____

# Lesson 30

1. Write the major scale pattern below. (Use "W's" and "H's")

Begin  _____   _____   _____   _____   _____   _____   _____

2. Color the houses blue in the G major scale beginning on open G.

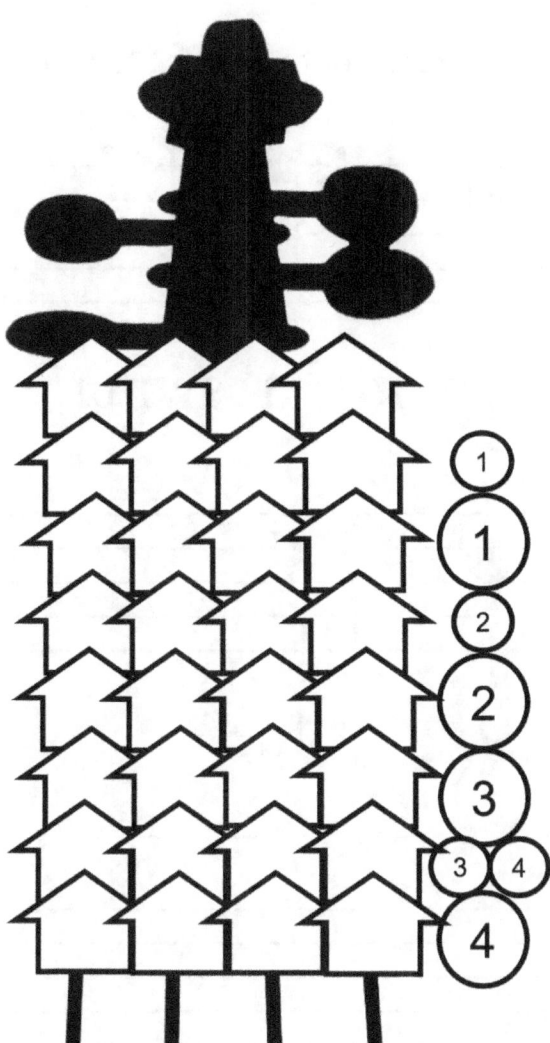

3. How many houses did you color? _____

4. How many sides does an octagon have? _____

5. How many tentacles does an octopus have? _____

An interval of 8 notes is called an **octave**. The prefix "oct" comes from the Greek language and means "eight." An octave covers eight letters. It is important to know that the first note and last note of an **octave** are the same letter.

  A to A = **octave**    D to D = **octave**    G to G = **octave**

6. Find another "G" on the fingerboard and color that house green. (Hint: it's on the E string!)

From "open G" up to 3rd finger "G" on the D string is one octave. From 3rd finger "G" on the D string up to low 2 "G" on the E string is another octave.

7. Beginning on 3rd finger on the D string, color the houses green in the G major scale.

This is called a 2-octave scale. It covers 2 octaves!

8. Draw the notes for the 2 octave G major Scale on the staff using whole notes.

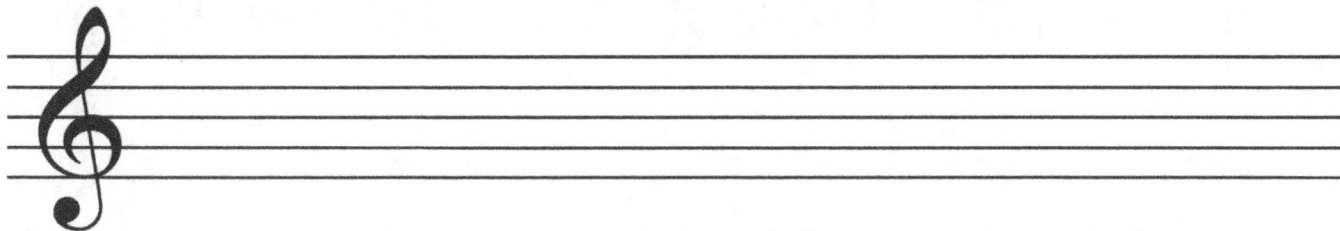

9. Write the letters under each note of the 2 octave scale.

10. Do any notes have a sharp?    yes       no     If yes, what letter? _____

(circle one)

When we use notes from a scale to compose a song, we say that the song is in the "key of
_____" (name of the scale.) This song "The Swing" is in the key of G because we are using
notes from the G scale.

11. Choose notes from the 2 octave G scale to compose the 2nd half of this song. Write the
letters in the blanks. Then, draw that pitch on the staff using the note value under the
blank. Remember to add sharps by any F's that you use.

## The Swing

Words: Robert Louis Stevenson

The Magic of Music Theory Book 2 - © 2025 Horsehair Music. Photocopying prohibited.

12. Write on the line if the example is a tie or a slur.

        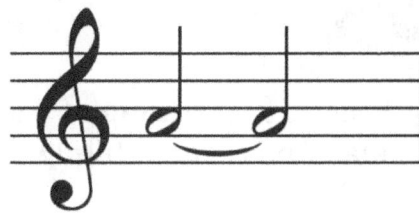

_____        _____        _____

_____        _____        _____

13. Write the interval (2nd, 3rd, or 8th) for each set of notes.

_____        _____        _____        _____

_____        _____        _____        _____

14. Write the definition in the blank for each tempo mark.

Presto _____

Prestissimo _____

Andante _____

Adagio_____

Allegro _____

Ritardando_____

**Definition Options:**
Fast
Very slow
Very fast
Very, very fast
Skipping along
Walking speed
Crawling speed
Gradually slowing down
Gradually speeding up
Gradually getting softer

# What do you hear? #9

Listen to a recording of Bachianas Brasileiras No. 4, I. Prelude by Brazilian composer Hector Villa Lobos [Vee-luh Low-boose] and answer the questions.

1. Is this in major or minor? _____ Is this piece slow or fast? _____

   Do you hear legato, staccato or both? _____

2. You will hear a rhythm pattern on open D. You may hear quarter notes, half notes, dotted half notes or whole notes. Write the notes that you hear in the order that you hear them.

3. Write the articulations and dynamics you hear. Mark staccato dots on the notes you hear that are short. If you hear legato, draw slurs connecting the notes that are slurred. Finally, mark in any crescendos or diminuendos that you hear. You will hear the example 4 times. Choose 1 thing to listen for each time the example is played.

The teacher may choose from these examples for question 2 or create their own.

For question 3 the teacher may choose from these examples or add their own articulations and dynamics.

The Magic of Music Theory Book 2 - © 2025 Horsehair Music. Photocopying prohibited.

# Lesson 31

1. Write the letter name for each note.

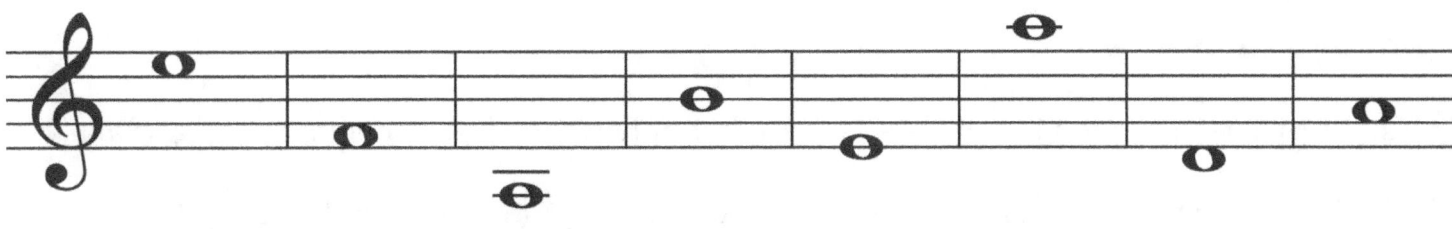

_____ _____ _____ _____ _____ _____ _____

_____ _____ _____ _____ _____ _____ _____

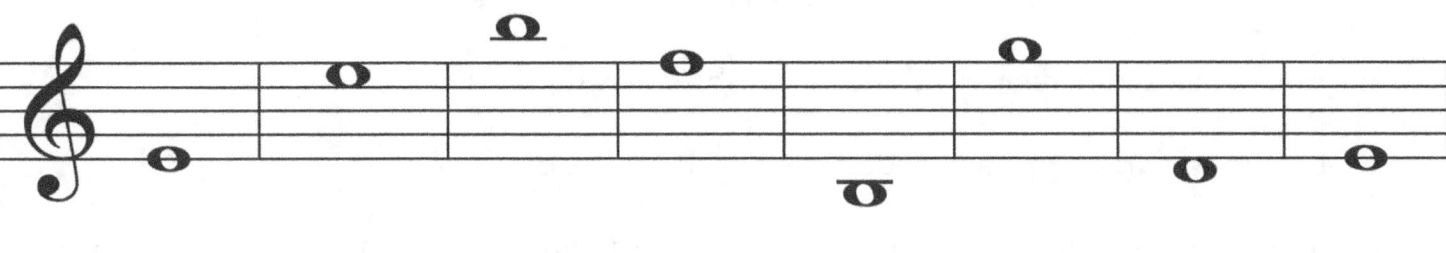

_____ _____ _____ _____ _____ _____ _____

2. Color all the houses on the fingerboard that match the letter on the scroll.

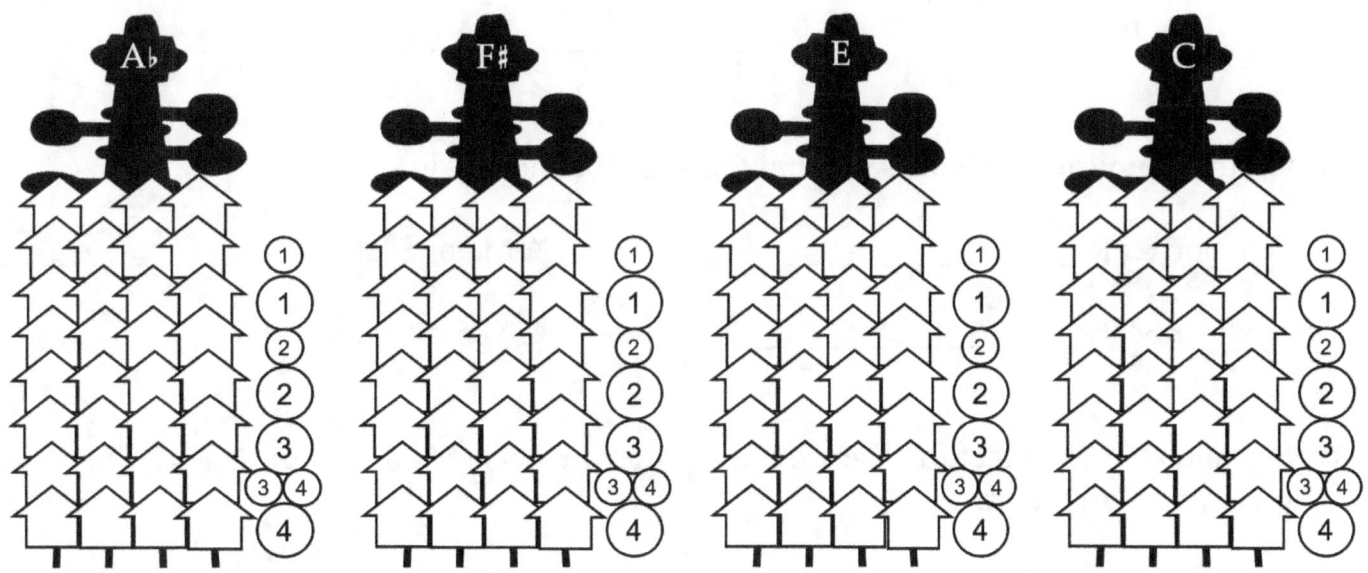

3. Draw the note on the staff. Don't forget the chromatic sign.

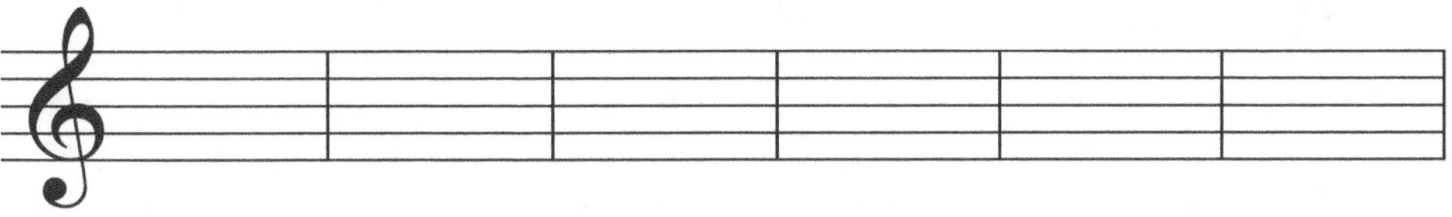

B♮        F♯        G♭        A♭        E♯        C♮

4. How many notes (or letters) are in an octave? _____

5. The distance between 2 notes is called an _____.

Circle the correct answer

6. An interval is measured by:  inches      number of letters      centimeters      fingernails

7. A string orchestra has:    only violins      woodwinds and strings      only strings

8. The person who leads the orchestra is called:    conductor      leader      coach

9. The person leading a section of the orchestra is called:    leader    conductor    principle

10. The little line that extends the staff is called:    ladder line      note line      ledger line

11. Legato is marked by using:    dot      dash      slur      tent

12. Staccato is marked by using:    dot      dash      slur      tent

13. A half step is marked by using:  dot      dash      slur      tent

14. Term that means to gradually slow down:    ritardando      crescendo      diminuendo

15. Write the major scale pattern:

  Begin  _____    _____    _____    _____    _____    _____    _____

16. On the line write the letters that have sharps for each scale.

   G Major Scale: _____        A Major Scale: _____

   D Major Scale: _____        C Major Scale: _____

17. Say and clap each picture. Decide if the pattern you clap is ♩ ♫ or ♫ ♩ . Then, draw the pattern on the line.

 **Bumble Bee**         **Birthday Cake**         **Ice Skating**

_____    _____    _____

## 18. Write the missing top number of the time signature.

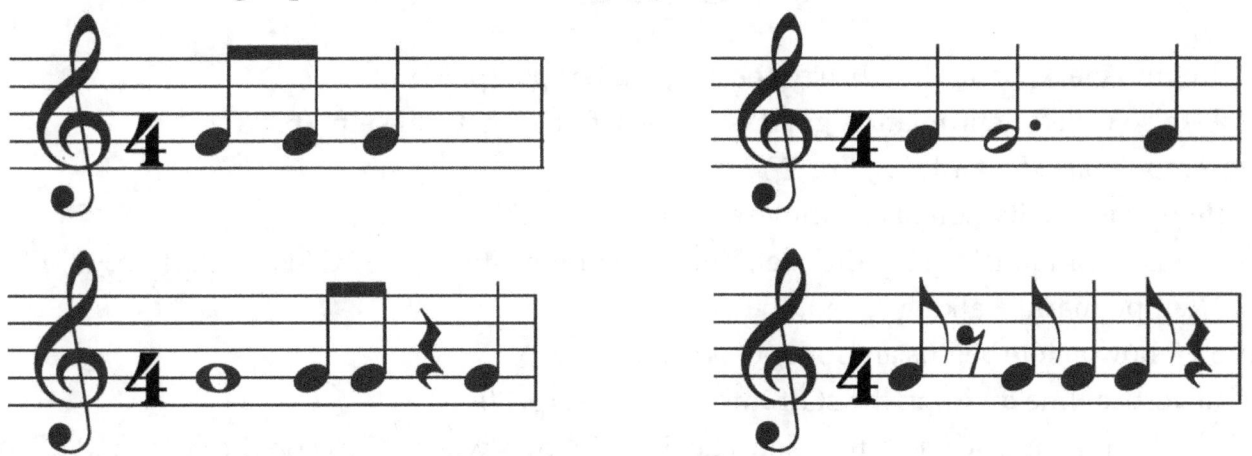

## 19. Draw the missing bar lines and double bar line.

Fanny Mendelssohn-Hensel, Adagio for Violin and Piano in E Major

## 20. Draw the symbol in each each box.

| Diminuendo | Crescendo | Legato  |
|---|---|---|
| Down Bow & Up Bow | Hooked Bow  | Staccato  |
| Natural | Sharp | Flat |

# Glossary

**a tempo** – [tempo mark; Italian] Return to the original tempo. (p. 35)

**Accidental** – also called a chromatic sign. It is a sharp, flat, or natural sign. (p. 53)

**Adagio** – [tempo mark; Italian] slow (p. 35)

**Allegro** – [tempo mark; Italian] fast, happy with energy (p. 35)

**Alto Clef** – violas read music using this clef. The C-clef points to where "C" is on staff. (p. 12, 13)

**Andante** – [tempo mark] walking speed. (p. 35)

**Articulation** – how a note begins and/or ends. (p. 56)

**Bar Line** – a vertical line dividing the staff into measures. (p. 20)

**Bass Clef** – cellos read music using this clef. The F-Clef shows where "F" is on the staff. (p. 12, 13)

**Baton** – a stick waved by a conductor to shows how fast or slow to play. (p. 7)

**Beam** – a horizontal line connecting the top of the stems to make eighth notes. (p. 26, 29, 58)

**Chromatic Half Step** – two notes that are a half step apart and use the same letter. (p. 46, 48, 51, 53, 61)

**Chromatic Sign** – a sharp, flat, or natural. It alters a note by one half step. (p. 41, 42, 43, 53)

**Concertmaster** – the person sitting first chair in the first violin section. Sometimes leads the
orchestra if there is no conductor. (p. 8)

**Conductor** – the person who leads the orchestra. (p. 7)

**Crescendo** – [dynamic sign; Italian] Grow gradually louder. (p. 17, 18)

**Da Capo al Fine** – [Italian] go back to the beginning and play up to where "Fine" is printed.
Abbreviated D.C. al Fine. (p. 23)

**Decrescendo** – [dynamic sign; Italian] Grow gradually softer. Synonym: diminuendo. (p. 17, 18)

**Diminuendo** – [dynamic sign; Italian] Grow gradually softer. Synonym: decrescendo. (p. 17, 18)

**Dotted Half Note** – gets 3 beats in 4/4 time. (p. 19)

**Double Bar Line** – a thin line followed by a thick line. Shows the end of a piece. (p. 20)

**Down Bow** – moving the bow from frog toward the tip. (p. 56)

**Dynamics** – volume. Tells how loud or soft to play. Dynamics are written using Italian words. (p. 16)

**Eighth Note** – a note with 1 flag. Gets half of a beat. Two eighth notes beamed together share 1 beat.
(p. 26, 27, 29, 58)

**Eighth Rest** – a rest showing silence for ½ a beat. (p. 31)

**Enharmonic** – two notes that sound the same but have different letter names. (p. 62, 82)

**Fine** – [Italian] the end. (Pronounced fee-neh) (p. 23)

**Flat** – a chromatic sign that lowers a note by 1 half step. (p. 41, 43, 46, 53)

**Forte** – [dynamic sign; Italian] loud. (p. 16)

**Fortissimo** – [dynamic sign; Italian] very loud. (p. 16)

**Forward Repeat Sign** – a thick line followed by a thin line and then two dots on either side of the
middle line. It shows the beginning of the section to be repeated. (p. 23)

**Half Note** – gets 2 beats in 4/4 time. (p. 19)

**Half Rest** – rest for 2 beats in 4/4 time. Looks like a hat. (Tip: *Hat* and *Half* both start with "H") (p. 19)

**Half Step** – closest distance between two notes; fingers are close together on the fingerboard.
(p. 38, 46, 61)

**Hooked Bow** – play 2 or more notes on one bow stroke, stopping the bow between the notes. Shown in the music with a staccato dot above each note and a slur connecting the first note of the stroke to the last note. (p. 57, 80)

**Interval** – the distance between two notes. Must include the first pitch when counting. (p. 84, 86)

**Key note** – first note of a scale; also called the tonic. (p. 63, 64)

**Largo** – [tempo mark; Italian] very slow. (p. 35)

**Ledger Line** – a small line that extends the staff. It can be above or below the 5 staff lines. (p. 12)

**Legato** – smooth and connected; marked with a slur. (p. 56)

**Major** – a tool composers use to create a mood. Major sounds happy or cheerful. (p. 55)

**Measure** – space on the staff between bar lines. (p. 20)

**Mezzo Forte** – [dynamic sign; Italian] medium loud. Softer than forte, but louder than mezzo piano. (p. 16)

**Mezzo Piano** – [dynamic mark; Italian] medium soft. Louder than piano, but softer than mezzo forte. (p. 16)

**Minor** – a tool composers use to create a mood. Minor sounds sad, scared, or even angry. (p. 55)

**Mosso** – [Italian] motion (p. 81)

**Natural** – a chromatic sign that cancels a flat or sharp. (p. 41, 46, 53)

**Octave** – an interval covering 8 letters, or 8 notes. (p. 87)

**Off Beat** – the second half of a beat that is weaker than the numbered beat. (p. 32)

**Piano** – [dynamic sign; Italian] soft. (p. 16)

**Pianissimo** – [dynamic sign; Italian] very soft. (p. 16)

**Piú** – [Italian] more (p. 81)

**Poco** – [Italian] little (p. 81)

**Poco piú mosso** – [Italian] literally, a little more motion. Increase the tempo a little bit. (p. 81)

**Presto** – [tempo mark; Italian] very fast (p. 35)

**Prestissimo** – [tempo mark; Italian] very very fast. (p. 35)

**Principle** – leader of a section in the orchestra. (p. 8)

**Quarter Note** – gets 1 beat in 4/4 time. (p. 19)

**Quarter Rest** – rest for 1 beat in 4/4 time. (p. 19)

**Ragtime** – a type of American music that uses syncopation and emphasizes the off-beat. (p. 33)

**Repeat Sign** – a thin line followed by a thick line with two dots on either side of staff line 3. Play that section again. (p. 23)

**Ritardando** – [tempo mark; Italian] gradually slowing down. Abbreviated, ritard. or rit. (p. 35)

**Rhythm** – how long or short a note is. Rhythm is measured and counted in beats. (p. 19)

**Scale** – 8 consecutive pitches, following a pattern of whole steps and half steps. (p. 63, 64)

**Sharp** – a chromatic sign that raises a note by 1 half step. (p. 41, 42, 46, 53)

**Skip** – skip a finger on the fingerboard; skip a letter in the music alphabet; skip a line or a space. A skip on the staff is line note to line note or space note to space note. A skip is the interval of a 3rd. (p. 84)

**Slur** – a curved line that starts and ends just above or below the notehead. (p. 56, 57, 79)

**Staccato** – play short or detached; marked with a dot above or below the note head. (p. 56, 75, 81)

**Step** – the letter before or after a letter in the music alphabet. The line or space above or below a note on the staff. The finger number before or after a finger on the fingerboard. A step is an interval of a 2$^{nd}$. (p. 84)

**String Orchestra** – a group made up of only stringed instruments. (p. 7)

**Symphony Orchestra** – a group including string, woodwind, brass, and percussion instruments. (p. 7)

**Syncopation** – emphasizing the weak beat or off beat. (p. 32, 33, 40)

**Tempo** – speed; how fast or slow music is played. (p. 35)

**Tie** – a slur that connects a note on the same line or space of the staff. It tells you to add the values of the notes together. Hold the note for the sum of the note values. (p. 79, 80)

**Time Signature** – found at the beginning of a piece. The top number tells the number of beats in each measure. The bottom number tells what kind of note gets 1 beat. A 4 on the bottom means the quarter note gets one beat. (p. 20, 24)

**Tonic** – first note of a scale; may also be called the keynote. (p. 57)

**Treble Clef** – violins read music using the treble clef. Sometimes called the G clef because the clef points to where "G" is on the staff. (p. 12, 13)

**Up Bow** – moving the bow from the tip toward the frog. (p. 56)

**Whole Note** – gets 4 beats in 4/4 time. (p. 19)

**Whole Rest** – rest for 4 beats, or rest for the whole measure. (p. 19)

**Whole Step** – 2 half steps together; space between fingers on the fingerboard. (p. 38)

# Index of Composers

# Note Drill 1

Write the letter name in the top blank and which string the note is found on in the bottom blank.

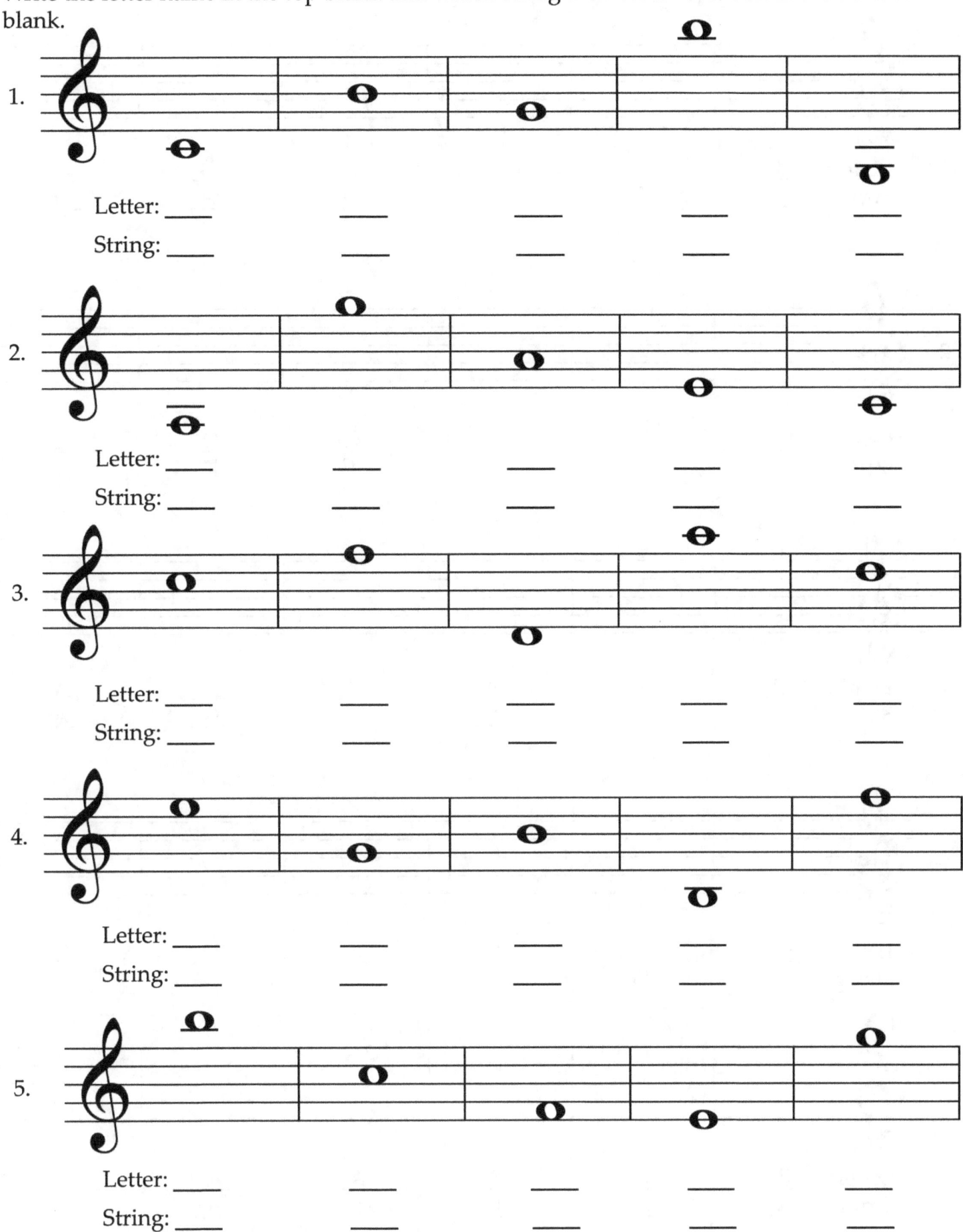

# Note Drill 2

Draw a whole note on the staff that matches the letter name on that string.

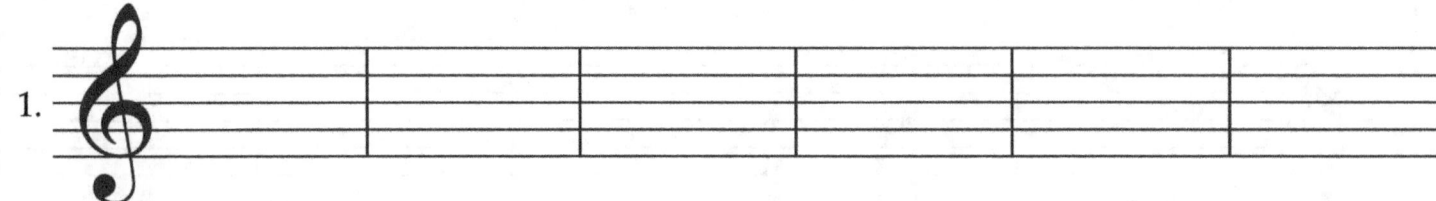

1.

| Letter: | B | C | A | G | B | E |
|---|---|---|---|---|---|---|
| String: | E | G | D | G | A | D |

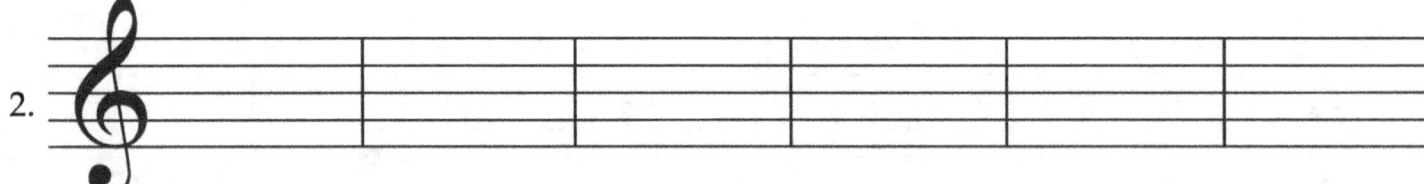

2.

| Letter: | F# | D | B | G# | D | G |
|---|---|---|---|---|---|---|
| String: | D | A | G | E | D | D |

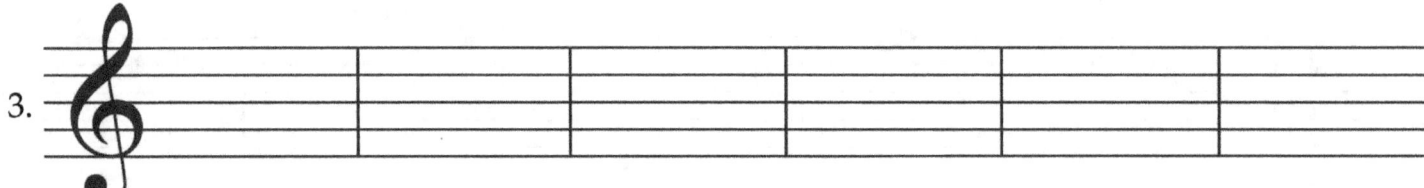

3.

| Letter: | C# | F# | A | E | A | A |
|---|---|---|---|---|---|---|
| String: | A | E | E | A | G | A |

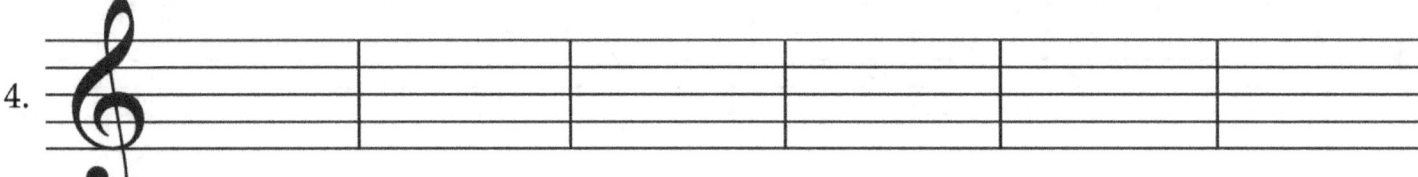

4.

| Letter: | C | E | D | F# | D | G |
|---|---|---|---|---|---|---|
| String: | G | D | A | E | G | D |

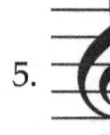

5.

| Letter: | B | B | B | A | A | A |
|---|---|---|---|---|---|---|
| String: | A | G | E | E | A | G |

# Note Drill 3

Write the letter name on the line under each note.

1.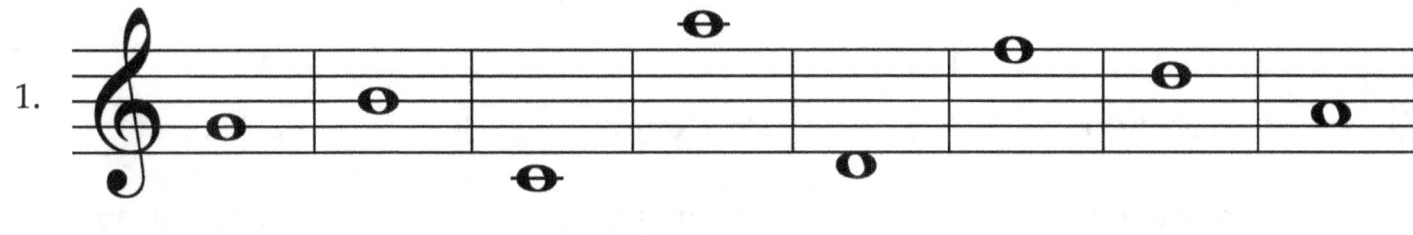

_____ _____ _____ _____ _____ _____ _____ _____

2.

_____ _____ _____ _____ _____ _____ _____ _____

3.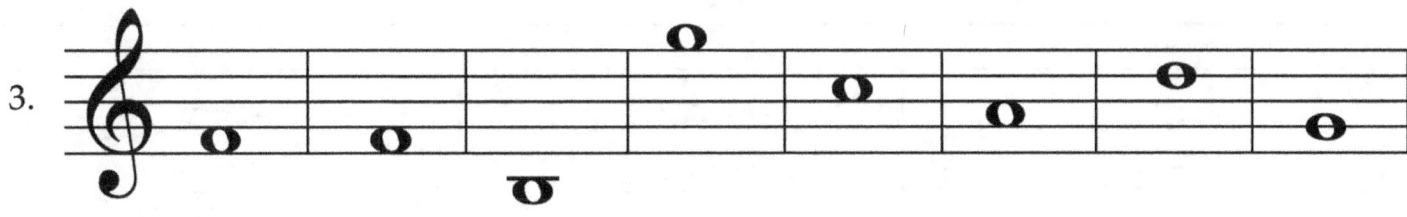

_____ _____ _____ _____ _____ _____ _____ _____

4.

_____ _____ _____ _____ _____ _____ _____ _____

5.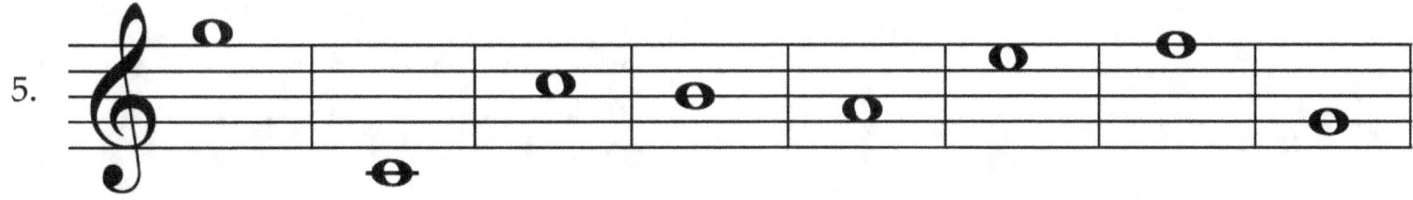

_____ _____ _____ _____ _____ _____ _____ _____

6.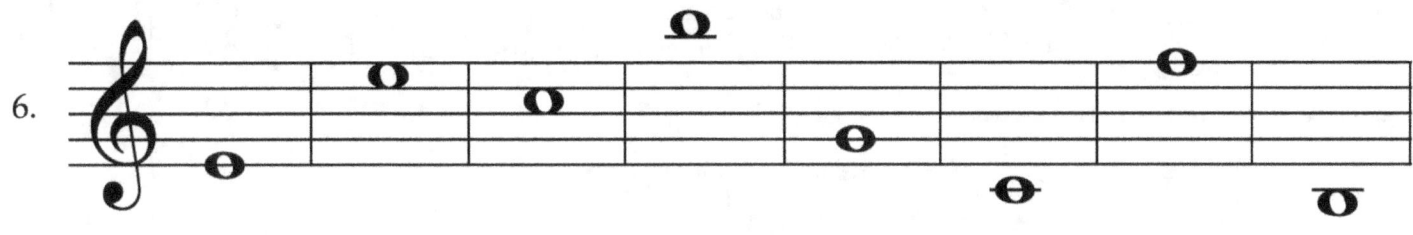

_____ _____ _____ _____ _____ _____ _____ _____

# Extra Ear Training Practice A: Dynamics

You will hear crescendo, diminuendo or both. Circle the dynamic you hear.

1.
**Crescendo**
**Diminuendo**
**Both**

2.
**Crescendo**
**Diminuendo**
**Both**

3.
**Crescendo**
**Diminuendo**
**Both**

4.

5.

6.

7.

8.

9.

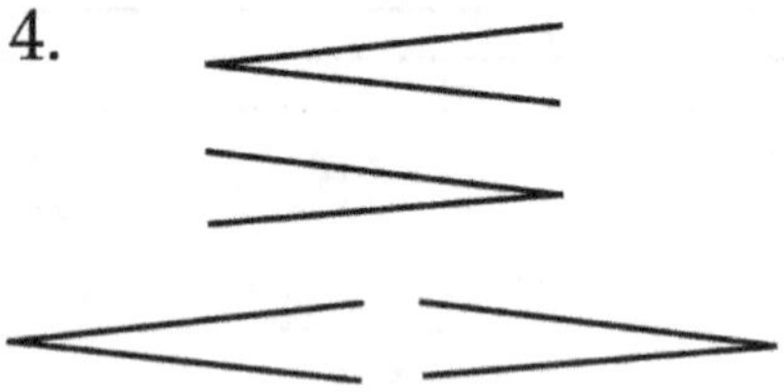

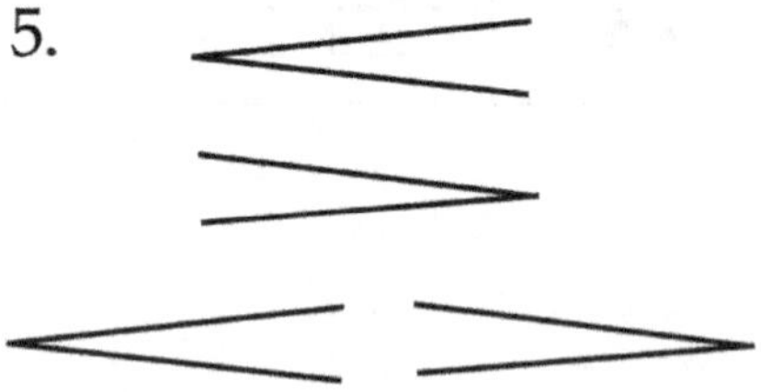

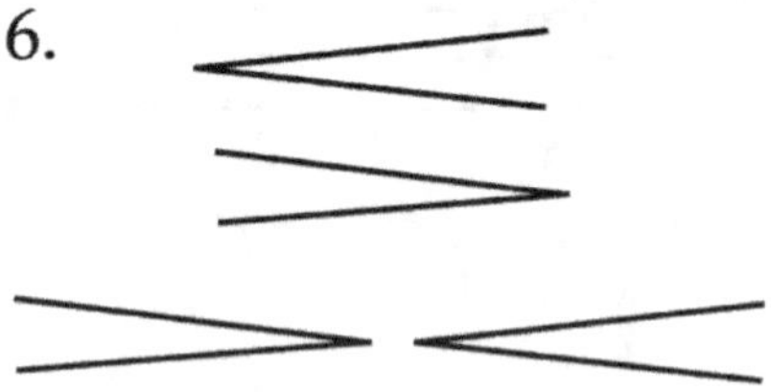

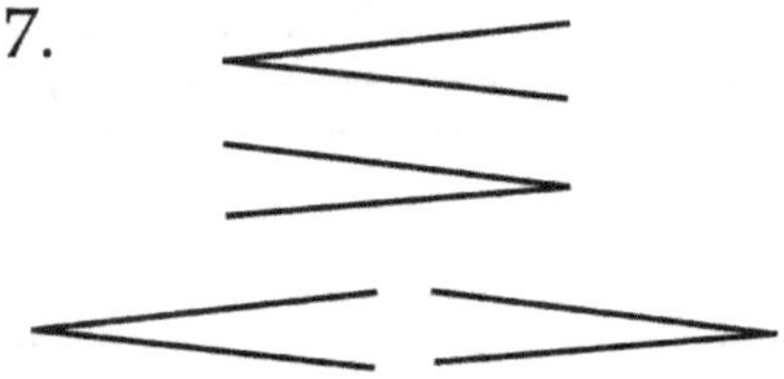

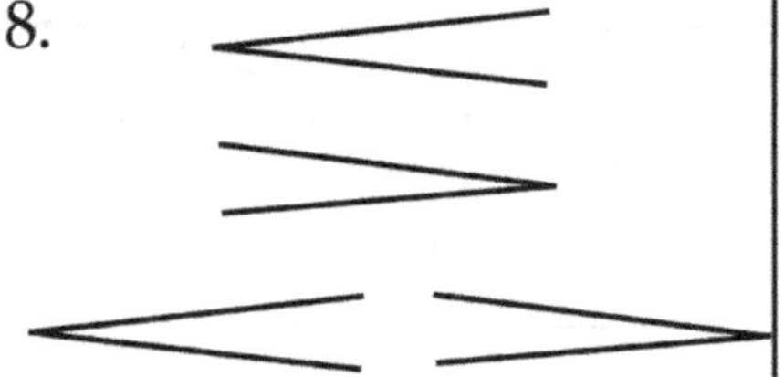

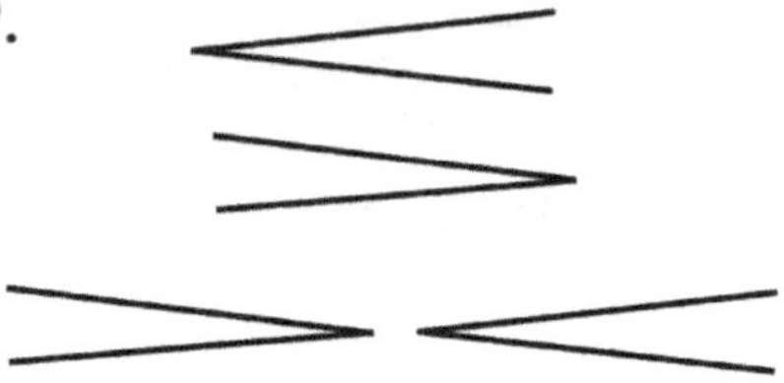

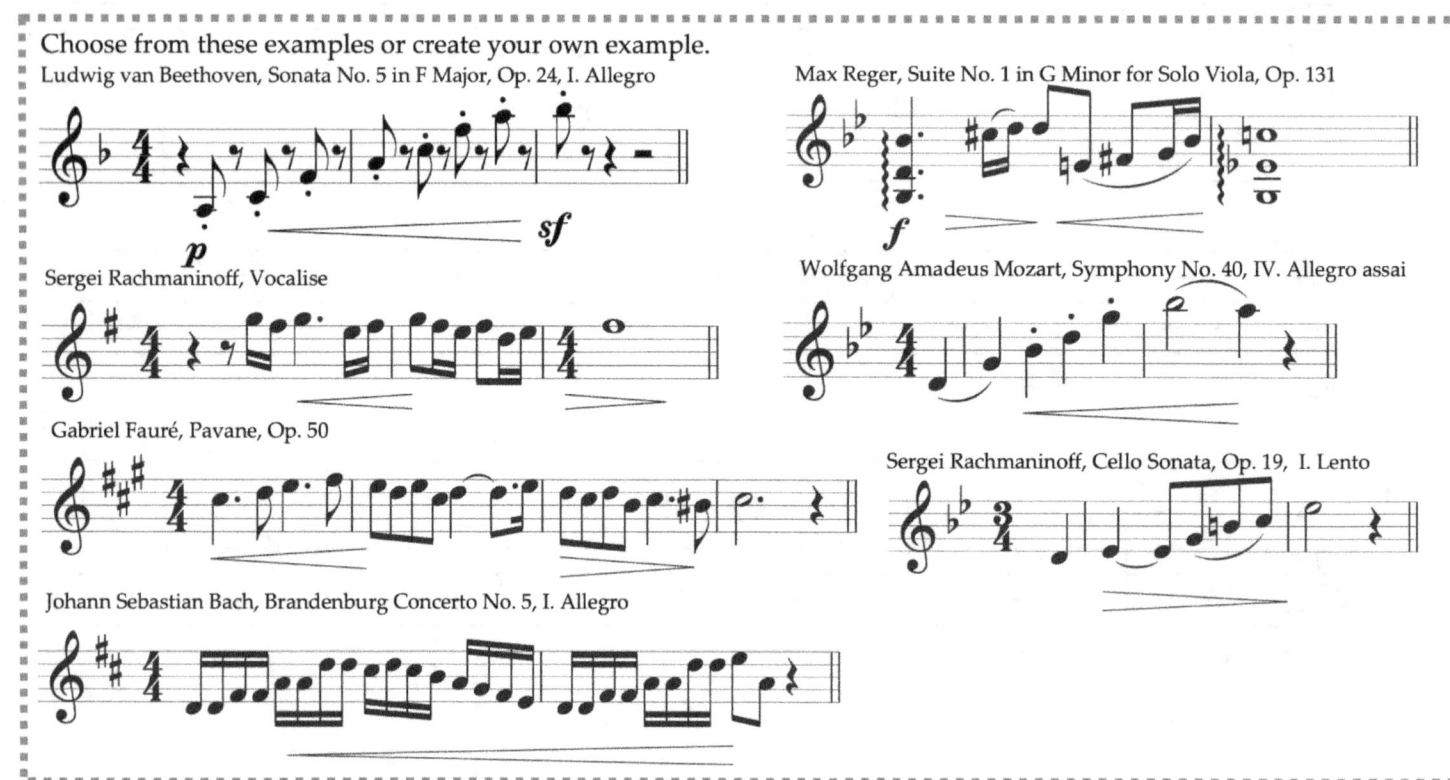

Choose from these examples or create your own example.

Ludwig van Beethoven, Sonata No. 5 in F Major, Op. 24, I. Allegro

Max Reger, Suite No. 1 in G Minor for Solo Viola, Op. 131

Sergei Rachmaninoff, Vocalise

Wolfgang Amadeus Mozart, Symphony No. 40, IV. Allegro assai

Gabriel Fauré, Pavane, Op. 50

Sergei Rachmaninoff, Cello Sonata, Op. 19, I. Lento

Johann Sebastian Bach, Brandenburg Concerto No. 5, I. Allegro

# Extra Ear Training Practice B: Rhythm Pattern

Circle the rhythm pattern you hear.

1.

2.
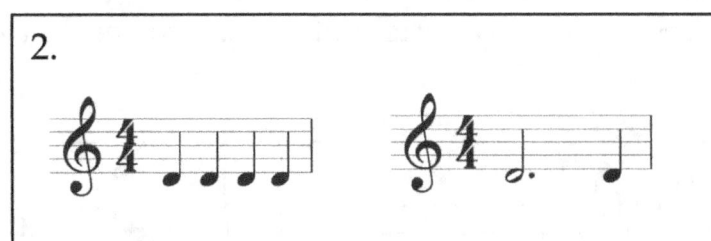

3.
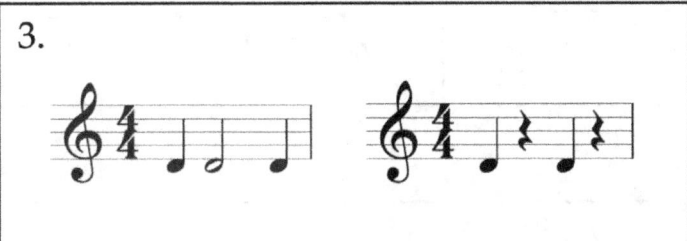

4.
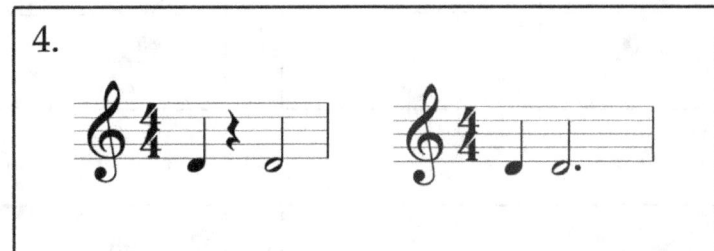

5.

6.
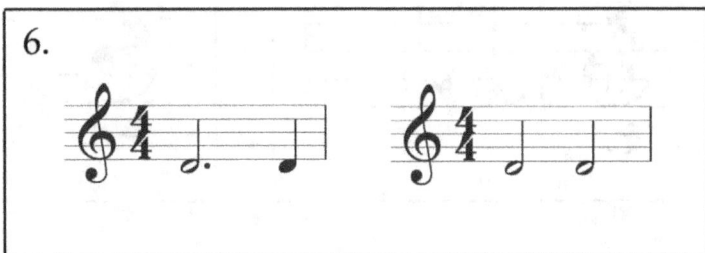

7.

8.

9.

10.

11.

12.

Choose one rhythm pattern from each box to play.

# Extra Ear Training Practice C: Step Up, Step Down, Repeat

You will hear 3 notes. The first two are given to you. The third note will step up, step down, or repeat. Draw a quarter note on the correct line or space in each measure.

Play the two notes in the measure and then choose a pitch that steps up, steps down or repeats.

# Extra Ear Training Practice D: Major or Minor

You will hear 5 notes stepping up. If the notes you hear are major, circle major and the happy face emoji. If the 5 notes you hear are minor, circle minor and the sad face emoji.

| | | | | |
|---|---|---|---|---|
| 1.  MINOR / MAJOR | 2.  MINOR / MAJOR | 3.  MINOR / MAJOR | 4.  MINOR / MAJOR | 5. MINOR / MAJOR |
| 6.  MINOR / MAJOR | 7.  MINOR / MAJOR | 8.  MINOR / MAJOR | 9.  MINOR / MAJOR | 10.  MINOR / MAJOR |

Choose from these examples or use your own example.

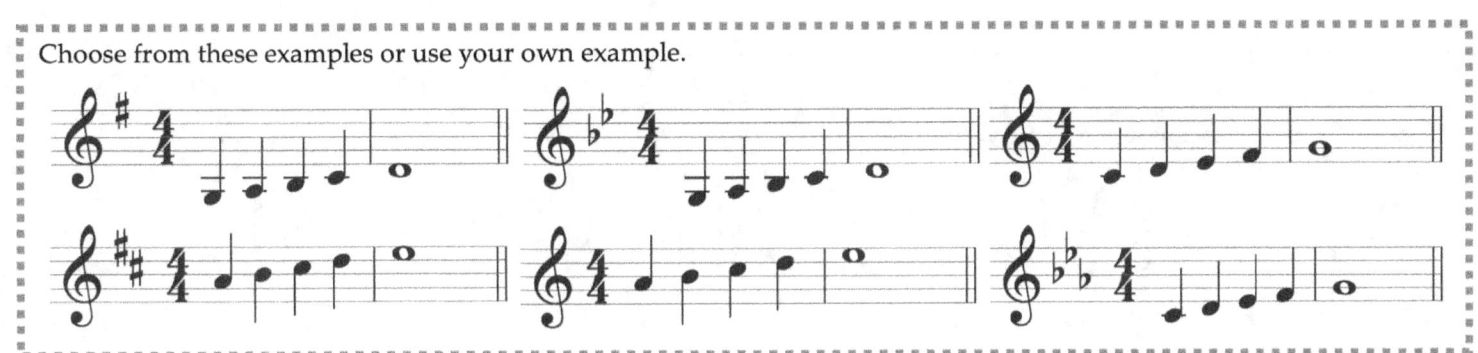

# Extra Ear Training Practice E: Rhythm Writing

You will hear a rhythm pattern on open D. You may hear quarter notes, half notes, dotted half notes or whole notes. Write all the notes you hear in the order that you hear them.

1.

$\frac{4}{4}$

2.

$\frac{4}{4}$

3.

$\frac{4}{4}$

4.

$\frac{4}{4}$

5.

$\frac{4}{4}$

Choose from these examples or create your own.

The Magic of Music Theory Book 2 - © 2025 Horsehair Music. Photocopying prohibited.

# Extra Ear Training Practice F: Articulation

Write the articulations and dynamics you hear. Mark **staccato dots** on the notes you hear that are short. If you hear legato, draw **slurs** connecting the notes that are slurred. Finally, mark in any **crescendos** or **diminuendos** that you hear. You will hear the example 4 times.
(Hint: Choose 1 thing to listen for each time the example is played.)

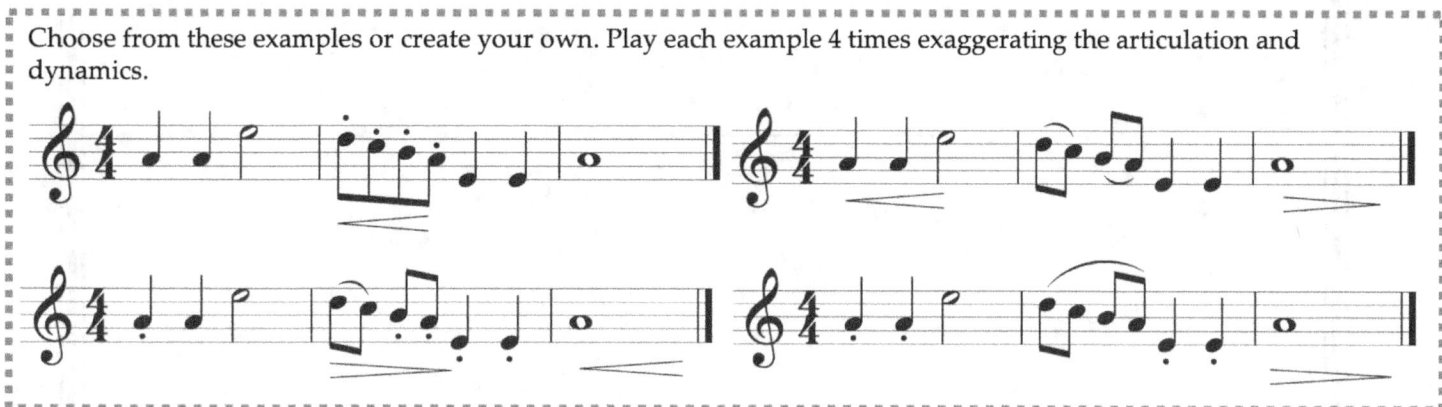

# Hooray!

_____

has completed

# The Magic of Music Theory
# Book 2

### and is now ready for Book 3

_____

(Teacher)

_____

(Date)

a tempo

ritardando

Prestissimo

Syncopation

Enharmonic

*ff*

*pp*

Very Fast

Gradually slowing down

Return to previous tempo

Tie -
add the note values together and hold

Same sound, different letters, different place on the staff

Emphasize the off beat or weak beat

Pianissimo
Very Soft

Fortissimo
Very Loud

Half Step Mark

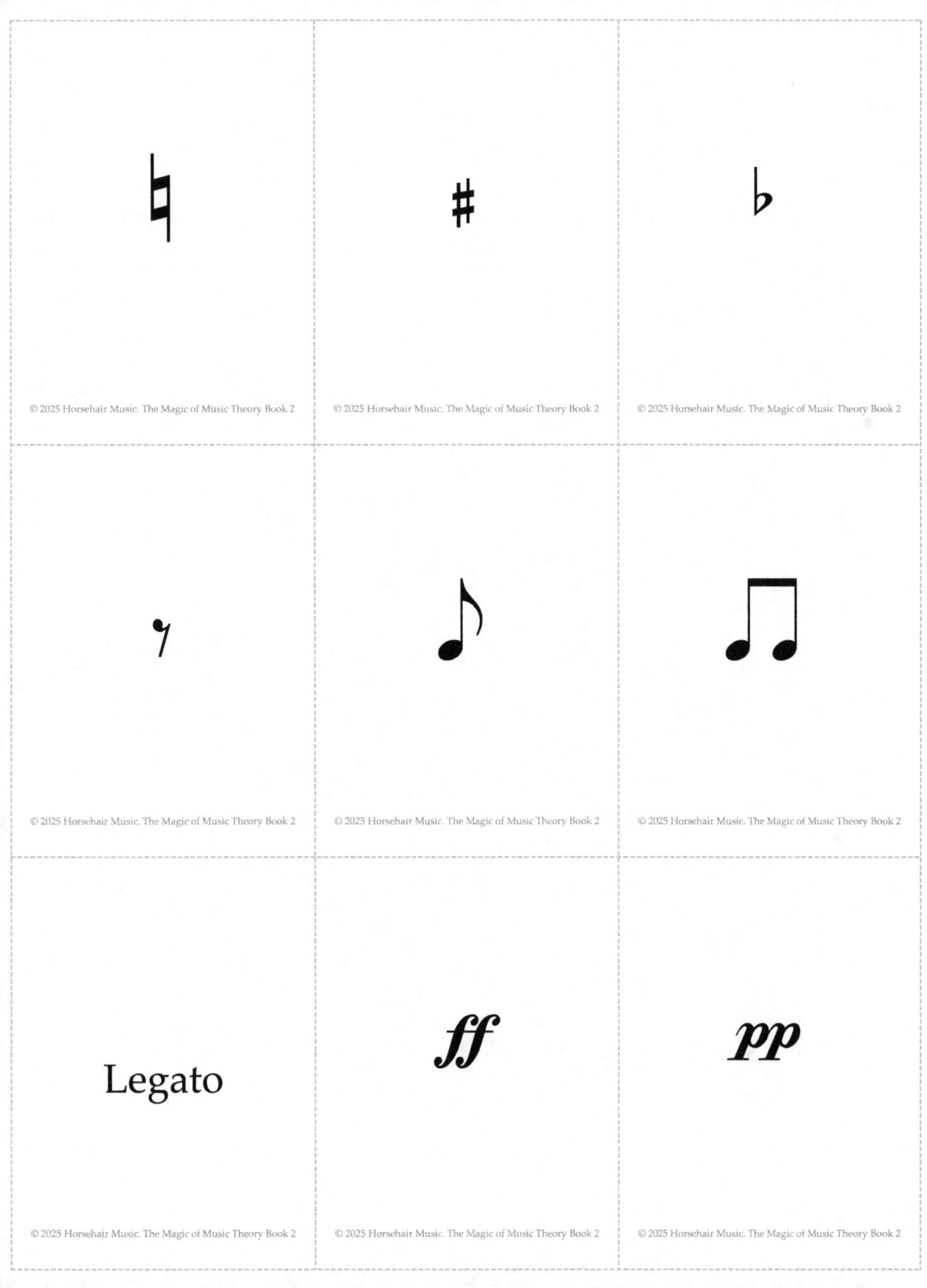

Legato

*ff*

*pp*

Flat

Lowers a pitch by a half step

Sharp

Raises a pitch by a half step

Natural

Cancels a flat or sharp

2 Eighth notes

Together they share 1 beat; each note gets ½ a beat

Eighth Note

½ a beat

Eighth Rest

½ a beat

Pianissimo
Very Soft

Fortissimo
Very Loud

Smooth and connected

# D.C. al Fine

# Fine

# Interval

# Octave

Interval?

Interval?

Repeat Sign

Play that section again

Hooked Bow

Play 2 notes on 1 bow stopping between notes.

Staccato

Play the notes short and detached

The distance between two notes

Finish or The End

Da Capo al Fine

Go back to the beginning and play to the Fine (finish).

2nd

3rd

Interval of 8 notes.

www.ingramcontent.com/pod-product-compliance
Lightning Source LLC
Chambersburg PA
CBHW081537120626
46550CB00009B/2762